The American Economic Impact on Canada

Hugh G. J. Aitken, John J. Deutsch,
W. A. Mackintosh, Clarence L. Barber,
Maurice Lamontagne, Irving Brecher,
Eugene Forsey

PUBLISHED FOR THE

Duke University Commonwealth-Studies Center

DUKE UNIVERSITY PRESS, DURHAM, N. C.

CAMBRIDGE UNIVERSITY PRESS, LONDON

1959

© 1959, Duke University Press

Cambridge University Press, London, N.W. 1, England

Library of Congress Catalogue Card Number
59-10916

Second printing, 1960

PRINTED IN THE UNITED STATES OF AMERICA
BY THE SEEMAN PRINTERY, INC., DURHAM, N. C.

Duke University Commonwealth-Studies Center Publications

PUBLICATION NUMBER 12

Duke University Commonwealth-Studies Center

The American Economic Impact on Canada

FOREWORD

THE APPEARANCE in the era of two World Wars of the Commonwealth of Nations as the heir to what was once the British Empire has not been given in the United States the attention it merits as a field for study. It was in response to this need that a Commonwealth-Studies Center was created at Duke University in 1955 with financial assistance from the Carnegie Corporation. The Center is devoted to the encouragement of research in Commonwealth affairs by members of the Duke University faculty and graduate students, and to the encouragement of similar research in economics, history, and political science by scholars and graduate students from various Commonwealth countries.

The purposes of the Center are implemented in a number of ways. Among these is the annual program known as the Commonwealth Summer Seminar and Research Group, which in each of the summers of 1956, 1957, and 1958 brought to the University for a period of two months groups of scholars already known for their interest and competence in one or another aspect of Commonwealth affairs. During the summer these scholars in residence pursued their own research in their chosen fields. They came together daily around the coffee table for informal discussion of their research projects or of more general Commonwealth topics. In addition, the group met formally at intervals as a seminar for critical analysis of papers prepared by distinguished visiting Canadian and American lecturers.

In the summer of 1958 the visting lecturers presented papers on the American economic impact on Canada. In these more formal sessions, as well as in the daily informal meetings, the visiting scholars were joined by interested members of the Duke University faculty.

The Summer Seminar and Research Group program has thus sought to further a number of useful purposes. It has provided a means whereby a limited number of scholars who are university teachers with Commonwealth interests may pursue their research throughout a summer unimpeded by the demands of classroom instruction. It has given them an opportunity for informal association with others of similar interests for the free exchange and stimulation of ideas. Finally, in centering attention on a particular theme during a given summer, it has brought to the Seminar, and to the wider audience to which these pages are addressed, some of the mature thought of scholars whose understanding of economic forces, as these have been operating between Canada and the United States, is penetrating as well as comprehensive.

Since the Commonwealth-Studies Center is concerned exclusively with the encouragement of research, any interpretations of Commonwealth developments appearing in its publications do not represent expressions of the views of the Center or of the Carnegie Corporation; the authors of the several publications are responsible for the conclusions expressed in them.

PAUL H. CLYDE, *Chairman*
The Summer Seminar and
Research Group

INTRODUCTORY STATEMENT

THE ECONOMIC RELATIONS between Canada and the United States constitute a unique and interesting problem for study. Nowhere else in the world are there two major nations with economies so similar and with such a long and open border between them. In such a situation, what economic problems arise between the two countries? How and why do the problems develop and how are they solved?

There is a long tradition of friendly relations and good will between the two countries. For this there are several obvious and valid reasons. To a considerable extent the two peoples have a common background and share the same political philosophy. With one important exception they speak the same language and share the same general culture. Their economic institutions are very similar and both economies have developed rapidly, although at different speeds. Many of the same economic problems, especially those arising out of geography, have faced the two countries and at times each has profited from the other's experience in dealing with them.

Despite these numerous and significant similarities there are a number of differences. By far the most important is the great difference in size. While in area Canada is considerably larger, the population of the United States is more than ten times that of Canada. In income and industrial strength the differences are even greater. Canadians have been much more aware of these differences than Americans, and quite understandably so, for in several respects they place Canadians at a distinct economic disadvantage. Canadians differ from Americans also in their political institutions. They remained longer under the close control of Britain and are still a member of the British Commonwealth of Nations. For a long time they were not a fully sovereign and independent nation, especially in their foreign relations. There is no revolutionary tradition in their political thought and they are more influenced by British precedents. Perhaps this is not so important in *what* they do as in *how* they do it. Another difference is that, economically, the United States has developed somewhat more rapidly than Canada, partly for geographical reasons. Frequently the Canadians have found themselves a decade or more behind the Americans in the development of water and rail transportation, of natural resources, and of industry. At times this has been a source of irritation to Canadian leaders for two reasons. First, it caused discontent among Canadians because the contrast was obvious and the two peoples were living side by side under approximately similar conditions. Second, Canadians were often compelled to make a special effort to avoid falling further behind and suffering a still greater economic disadvantage. In other words, the Canadians sometimes felt that the economic achievements of the United States shaped the desires and goals of Canadians and thus influenced Canadian economic policies, and yet they were destined always to lag behind in that economic race. Finally, there is the difference that in Canada there is a large ethnic group which has never been assimilated into the prevailing culture and economic practices of the country. In the United States there have been larger and more numerous racial groups but, with one exception, they have been more rapidly assimilated.

Because of these numerous differences the border between the United States and Canada *does* make a difference. A very large majority of Americans, mainly because their interests are centered elsewhere, are either ignorant of these differences or tend to treat them lightly and of no consequence. But, as noted above, Canadians have been more aware of them and more concerned about them. In earlier days the principal sources of concern were military and political. Canadians were worried lest they be overrun and annexed by the United States. It is generally agreed that one of the major reasons for federation in 1867 was Canadian concern about the military capabilities and intentions of the United States. That fear found some basis of reality in the utterances of American demagogues; it did not disappear with the enactment of the British North American Act, but continued much longer than is generally realized. It was evident especially in the turbulent days when the western prairies were being settled. Now that fear has been dissipated. In the face of the cold war and the nature of modern warfare, the two countries are now one community and must survive or perish together. These circumstances have forced them to plan and implement a joint defense policy.

In recent years the causes of concern in the relations between the two countries have shifted more toward economic matters. This shift has approximately coincided with the attainment by Canada of the status of a fully independent and sovereign nation and of a position of considerable importance as a world power. As labor organizations gained greatly in strength and importance during the thirties, labor policies and organizations in Canada were influenced to a considerable extent by American practices. This was a matter of concern to many Canadians, especially those who looked askance at the growing strength of labor. More recently, and especially since World War II, attention has shifted to the effects of United States farm policies on Canadian agriculture and even more to the growing American penetration into the Canadian economy as represented by a steadily rising flood of investment funds. This latter has caused much concern to many Canadian observers as American investors expanded their control over strategic Canadian industries and resources.

The papers in this volume were delivered and discussed at a Summer Seminar of the Duke University Commonwealth-Studies Center in the summer of 1958. The seminar was designed to afford a forum for the presentation and discussion of the most competent and authoritative Canadian opinion on the question of the American economic impact on Canada. The papers cover four main areas: (1) the effects of American influence on Canadian economic policy; (2) the repercussions of American farm policies on Canadian agriculture; (3) the extent and effects of American investments in Canada; and (4) the influence of American labor organizations and policies on Canadian labor. In addition there is one regional study of the American economic impact on Quebec.

By far the most important cause of concern to Canadians is the heavy and rising flow of investment funds from the United States. This is understandable for several reasons. First, it is a phenomenon which has developed rapidly in a short period of time and represents a sharp reversal from previous trends. For fifteen years—from 1930 to 1945—there was no increase in Canada's foreign debt; in fact, her *net* foreign debt declined by almost 50 per cent. Then in a period of twelve years the gross foreign debt increased by over 150 per cent. Second, United States investments increased greatly in proportion to

British investments. This often involved changes in trade connections and added to the already heavy deficit in Canadian payments to the United States. Third, as already noted, the investments were heavily concentrated in strategic industries and resources. This gives rise to concern about Canada's ability to control her economic resources for her own national purposes.

These are real and significant problems and it is understandable and proper that both Canadians and Americans should concern themselves with them. The following papers very ably describe the development of those problems and interpret their significance. But since the papers are concerned solely with the problems, it may not be out of place here to point out a few facts which afford some background or perspective against which they may be evaluated. First, it should be noted that much this same thing has happened before. Just before and just after World War I there was a heavy inflow of investment funds from abroad. While the absolute growth of foreign investment since World War II has been greater than in the whole period from 1900 to 1945, "The rate of increase was much greater before World War I, and . . . foreign capital financed a much larger part of total capital formation in previous periods of rapid growth than in the period since 1945."[1] In the period from 1900 to 1930, too, the amount of American funds coming in greatly exceeded British funds and the proportion of foreign investments held in England declined sharply.

Second, the figures on investments are in absolute amounts and in terms of a dollar which has depreciated a great deal in the past twenty years. In relation to other pertinent economic data the trends are quite different. Thus, "In 1926 to 1939, the net external debt was equal to a full year's GNP, and considerably more than this in the depression of the '30's. By 1948 it was only one-quarter of GNP, and while net debt has risen since then it was still less than one-third of GNP in 1955."[2] In the same way, the ratio of net interest and dividend payments on the foreign investments to GNP declined from 5.2 per cent in 1930 to 4.4 per cent in 1939 to 1.6 per cent in 1948 and to 1.2 per cent in 1955. The ratio of net interest

[1] Irving Brecher and S. S. Reisman, *Canada-United States Economic Relations* (Ottawa, 1957), p. 87.
[2] *Ibid.*, p. 87.

and dividend payments to Canada's total international receipts declined from 26.8 per cent in 1930 to 21.0 per cent in 1939 to 7.8 per cent in 1948 and then rose slightly to 8.2 per cent in 1955.[3] Thus in terms of the rate of increase and of the means of servicing the debt, the recent increase in the foreign debt has not been nearly as great as in former periods.

Further, as Professor Viner points out in a quotation given in one of the papers, the relations between the United States and Canada are quite different from those which have frequently prevailed in the past between lending and borrowing nations, especially between a wealthy country and an underdeveloped country. Generally, the American corporations operating in Canada have been good "citizens" and there have been no claims of flagrant abuses or exploitation by them. It is almost universally agreed that the great inflow of American funds has benefited both countries and has contributed greatly to the rapid pace of economic development which Canada has experienced in recent years.

In this connection several observers have made an interesting and perhaps significant comment. Almost every fear and complaint expressed in Canada about the inflow of American funds and the dominance of American corporations can find its counterpart in the southern region of the United States. There, too, there are complaints about "absentee ownership," about the absence of research facilities in the region, about the fact that able men must leave the region in order to hold the higher positions in the companies, and about the fact that under certain conditions the companies may tend to "drain profits" from the region. These facts seem to indicate that the problem is not a political or national one, but rather that it is purely economic in origin. Both Canada and the South were late in starting industrialization, and they must, along with the advantages, accept these superficial disadvantages which accompany the process of industrialization by outside companies. In the South, and no doubt in Canada also, the conditions are steadily, even if very slowly, changing; and eventually each of them may hope to be a mature and fairly autonomous industrial region.

Finally, as the concluding paper points out, it seems clear that regardless of what may have been true in earlier years, Canadian labor

[3] *Ibid.*, Table 21, p. 94.

organizations are now almost entirely self-sufficient and in control of their own policies. They are mature organizations with able leadership; their policies and procedures are based on the needs and desires of Canadian labor and not upon the wishes or practices of organizations in the United States.

These considerations do not mean that existing economic problems between the two countries are unimportant or should be treated lightly. They do indicate, however, that those problems are not unprecedented, that they are not of such a magnitude as to endanger the economy of either country, and that, given careful study and good will on both sides, they can be solved satisfactorily.

The authors of these papers are men who are widely known and highly respected in their fields. For the benefit of general readers, however, especially those in the United States, it may be appropriate here to supply a few words of identification. With one exception, all of the authors are Canadians. All of them are distinguished scholars who have demonstrated their analytical and writing abilities. Dr. Hugh G. J. Aitken is Assistant Professor of Economics in the Division of Social Sciences of the University of California at Riverside, Riverside, California. Dr. John J. Deutsch went from the academic world into the government service, where he filled several important positions, including that of Secretary to the Treasury Board and Assistant Deputy Minister of Finance; he is now Professor of Economics and Political Science in the University of British Columbia, Vancouver, British Columbia. Dr. W. A. Mackintosh for many years held a high post in the Department of Finance of the Canadian government and was a leading figure in shaping the economic policies of that government. He was the principal author of the 1945 White Paper on Employment and Income; he is now Principal and Vice Chancellor of Queen's University, Kingston, Ontario. Dr. Clarence L. Barber is Professor of Economics in the University of Manitoba, Winnepeg, Manitoba. Mr. Maurice Lamontagne has been Economic Advisor to the Privy Council. He is now Lecturer in Economics in the University of Ottawa, Ottawa, Ontario, and Special Assistant to the Hon. Lester B. Pearson, Head of the Liberal party and Leader of the Opposition in the Canadian Parliament. Dr. Irving Brecher is the author of several works on Canadian finance and co-author of one of the principal volumes prepared for the Royal Commission on

Canada's Economic Prospects. He is now Associate Professor of Economics in McGill University, Montreal, Quebec. Dr. Eugene Forsey is a former teacher of Political Science and is now Director of Research for the Canadian Labour Congress, Ottawa, Ontario.

Duke University   B. U. RATCHFORD

CONTENTS

TABLES

The American Economic Impact on Canada

The Changing Structure of the Canadian Economy

With Particular Reference to the Influence of the United States

HUGH G. J. AITKEN

I

Canada, from the beginning of its history, has been a vulnerable economy, exposed to pressures and stimuli from more advanced nations. Its development has been geared to external demands and external challenges. The early history of the Canadian maritimes is the story of the imperialistic rivalries of the nation states of Western Europe: France, Spain, Portugal, and Britain. The development of the St. Lawrence lowlands reflects the struggle between France and Britain for control over this vital avenue to the continental hinterland. The Pacific coast enters the history of the modern world as the scene of intense commercial and imperial rivalry between Russia, the United States, and Britain. And the western prairies, whether in the days of the fur trade or as "the wheat economy," developed primarily as a staple-producing region serving the industrialized economies of Western Europe. The nation that today is Canada has never been master of its own destiny; as a satellitic staple-producing economy, it reflected, and still reflects, in its rate of development the imperatives of more advanced areas.

The development of the Canadian economy has been the result of the responses, sometimes successful and sometimes not, to these external challenges. Not only the rate but also the character of Canada's economic growth reflects the dependent role it has played in relation to other areas. Normally the Canadian reaction to external pressures has been defensive in nature; the creation of a Canadian nation and of a Canadian economy in the second half of the nineteenth century was in fact the result of deliberate policy decisions taken to counteract the threat of absorption by a larger political and economic unit, in this case the United States. Canadian expansionism, in contrast to that of the United States, has always been defensive expansionism.

The response of one economic system to pressure exerted on it by another may be described as positive or creative if it results in an acceleration of the rate of economic development in the former; that is, if it results in an increase in national income and in income per capita. Canada today exists as a national economy because its reactions to external pressure have been predominantly positive. That this should be the case was not in any sense necessary or inevitable: it resulted from distinct political and economic decisions. The strategic decisions in the process of economic growth in Canada have historically been such as to promote the creation, integration, and growth of a national economy north of the United States boundary. The necessity for framing and implementing such decisions continues today to be among the primary preoccupations of Canadian governments.

II

The long-term trend of economic development in Canada may be visualized as a succession of S-shaped logistic curves, in which periods of rapid growth have alternated with periods of slower growth. In modern Canadian history, the periods of rapid growth have been three in number; the decade of the 1850's, the years from 1900 to 1913, and the period from 1939 to the present. Each of these periods saw marked changes in the structure of the Canadian economy; each was characterized by large imports of labor, capital, entrepreneurship, and technology from other countries; and each represented the implementation of a positive response to external pressure. The decade of the 1850's witnessed the economic integration of the St. Lawrence lowlands, the extension to its feasible limits of the agricultural frontier in southern Ontario, the beginning of manufacturing industry in Ontario and Quebec, and the completion of a railroad system extending from the Detroit River to the Atlantic seaboard. The years from 1900 to 1913 saw the agricultural settlement of the western prairies, the opening up of a mining frontier on the Canadian Shield, the development of the newsprint industry, and the beginnings of large-scale hydroelectric development in the area of the Great Lakes and the St. Lawrence. The period since 1939 has been characterized by remarkable industrial expansion in central Canada, the development of new resources of nonferrous metals and iron ore, the birth of important new industries in petroleum, natural gas, and petro-chemicals, and the construction of the St. Lawrence Seaway.

The periods that intervened between these successive spurts of accelerated growth were not phases of stagnation or decline, but rather breathing spells during which the structure of the economy was adjusted to the new levels of productivity made possible by the capital accumulation and innovations of the preceding period. Evidence of a rapid spurt of development in the 1850's lies in the volume of new investment in railroads, the large-scale importation of capital, heavy immigration, the buoyancy of government revenues, and the behavior of prices. Quantitative data become more readily available as we approach the twentieth century. Gross national product at constant prices appears to have grown at an annual rate of about 5 per cent in the 1870's and at a somewhat slower rate in the 1880's and 1890's. The turn of the century brought marked acceleration, the average annual rate of growth rising to about 8 per cent in the period 1900-1910.[1] This was matched briefly during the postwar prosperity of 1923-1928, but the onset of depression brought serious retardation and not until 1939 did the rate of growth revive. Between 1939 and 1954 GNP in constant (1935-1939) dollars increased from $5,664 million to $11,725 million, representing an average yearly rate of growth of approximately 5 per cent over the period.[2]

Growth in total physical output has been accompanied by marked increases in per capita income, in the degree of economic diversification, and in other standard indices of economic development. Income per capita (at constant prices) increased by 70 per cent between

[1] These data are drawn from Penelope Hartland, "Factors in Economic Growth in Canada," *Journal of Economic History*, XV (1955), 13-22, especially pp. 15-16. For estimates of gross national expenditure in constant dollars by decades for the period since 1867, see O. J. Firestone, *Canada's Economic Development, 1867-1953* (London, 1958), p. 66. For figures on GNP in current dollars since 1929, see Appendix Table 4.

[2] *Canada Year Book*, 1956, p. 1089, Table 3. Corresponding average rates of growth were 4 per cent per annum for the period 1926-1952, and 5 per cent for the period 1947-1952.

1926 and 1953, despite an increase in population of 56 per cent during the same period. In 1953 income per capita in Canada was estimated at $1,318 (in U. S. dollars of current purchasing power), as compared with $1,908 in the United States, $930 in the United Kingdom, and $921 in Australia.[3] Economic diversification can be measured in a variety of ways. Estimates of changes in the urban-rural distribution of the population for the period from 1871 to 1956 are given below in Table I. As a basis for comparison it may be noted that in the United States in 1950 the distribution was 64 per cent urban and 36 per cent rural.[4]

TABLE I

The Urban-Rural Distribution of Canada's Population, Selected Years, 1871-1956*

Year	Population (Thousands)	PERCENTAGE DISTRIBUTION		Year	Population (Thousands)	PERCENTAGE DISTRIBUTION	
		Urban	Rural			Urban	Rural
1871	3,689	19.5	80.5	1921	8,788	49.5	50.5
1881	4,325	25.6	74.4	1931	10,377	53.7	46.3
1891	4,833	31.8	68.2	1941	11,507	54.4	45.6
1901	5,371	37.5	62.5	1951	14,009	62.9	37.1
1911	7,207	45.4	54.6	1956	16,081	66.7	33.3

*The census definition of "rural" and "urban" changed in the 1951 Census. Before that date the fringes of major urban areas were classified as rural. The 1951 and 1956 censuses specify that all cities, towns, and villages of 1,000 and over, as well as all parts of census metropolitan areas and other major urban areas, are classified as urban. Since metropolitan area developments are a fairly recent phenomenon, the influence of these census changes probably decreases as one goes back in time.
Source: Dominion Bureau of Statistics, Census of Canada, 1951 and 1956.

Similar trends are evident from a classification of the labor force into primary, secondary, and tertiary occupations, as suggested by Colin Clark.[5] The percentage distribution for Canada in 1911 and 1955, and for the United States in 1955, are given in Table II.

III

This process of development, particularly during phases of rapid acceleration, has been greatly facilitated by the transfer to Canada of

[3] Charles P. Kindelberger, Economic Development (New York, 1958), p. 6, Table 1.1.
[4] United Nations Demographic Yearbook, 1955, Table 7, pp. 185-197.
[5] Colin Clark, The Conditions of Economic Progress (3rd ed.; London, 1957), especially chap. ix.

TABLE II

OCCUPATIONAL DISTRIBUTION OF THE LABOR FORCE, CANADA AND THE UNITED STATES

	Canada 1911	Canada 1955	U. S. A. 1955
Primary	39.4	21.1	14.2
Secondary	30.8	32.6	34.0
Tertiary	29.9	46.3	51.8

Percentages do not always add to 100 because of rounding.
Sources: *United Nations Demographic Yearbook, 1955*, Table 16; *Canada Year Book, 1955*, p. 1336.

capital, labor, technology, and entrepreneurship originating in other countries. It has also tended to mold the structure of the Canadian economy in such a way as to make it highly dependent on other countries as sources of capital and as markets for Canadian exports. It has resulted in a situation commonly described as one of dependence, vulnerability, or "openness." In the nineteenth century and until World War I the dependence was primarily on Great Britain, which was the principal market for Canadian exports—fish, fur, wheat, and timber—and also Canada's principal source of capital imports and immigrants. The United States in this period played the role of a disturbing element—a threat to the connection with Britain and to Canada's dominant orientation to the British market. After World War I, however, and particularly after 1926, the United States supplanted Britain as the dominant power in Canada's external economic relations. The shift of orientation is clearly evident in the statistics of Canada's foreign indebtedness. In 1914 British investment accounted for about three-quarters of all foreign capital in Canada. By the end of 1954 the proportion had fallen to less than one-fifth; the total at present is less in absolute terms than it was in 1914. United States investment in Canada, on the other hand, has increased both absolutely and relatively. By the early 1920's the United States had supplanted Britain as Canada's largest creditor, and by the end of 1955 United States investments accounted for 77 per cent of all foreign investments in Canada. Canada's net indebtedness to the United States increased from $2.8 billion to $8.9 billion between 1926 and 1955, while net indebtedness to Britain declined from $2.6 billion to $1.0 billion.[6]

[6] Irving Brecher and S. S. Reisman, *Canada-United States Economic Relations* (Ottawa, 1957), pp. 86-88. See Appendix Tables 8, 9, 10, and 11 for additional data on this point.

Dependence on the United States and susceptibility to influence by the United States go beyond the question of capital imports. As an economy still largely organized around the production of raw materials and foodstuffs, Canada's prosperity and rate of development depend upon access to foreign markets. Vulnerability to tariff policy and to changes in demand over which Canada can exercise no control are the consequences. Just as the state of the British market and changes in British tariff policy dominated the thinking of Canadian statesmen and businessmen in the early nineteenth century, so today the state of the United States market and changes in United States tariffs concern every Canadian in a direct and immediate way. Dependence on the United States in these respects also is increasing. In 1939 the United States absorbed about 40 per cent of Canada's exports and furnished about two-thirds of Canadian imports; the corresponding figures for Britain were 36 per cent and 15 per cent respectively. By 1957 the United States was buying about 60 per cent of Canada's exports and providing almost 75 per cent of Canada's imports, while the shares of Great Britain had fallen to 17 per cent and 9 per cent respectively.[7]

Is Canada, then, despite her high standard of living and productive economy, becoming more and not less dependent on other countries? Some at least of the evidence suggests a contrary view. Nonresident ownership of Canadian industry and commerce, as a whole, for example, has been substantially reduced in recent years. Before World War II nonresident ownership represented about 38 per cent of Canadian industry and commerce; by the end of 1954 the ratio had fallen to 32 per cent.[8] The ratio of foreign capital to total investments in Canada has been declining for a considerable period: the principal source of capital for Canadian development has for many years been Canadian in origin. Safarian and Carty, estimating the extent to which Canada has on balance drawn on the resources of other countries for the savings used for development, have concluded that in the period 1946-1954 savings by Canadians were large enough to finance all but 6 per cent of net capital formation.[9] The role of

[7] *Ibid.*, pp. 3-4. See Appendix Table 6 for data on the geographical distribution of Canada's imports and exports for other years.

[8] *Canada Year Book, 1955*, p. 1179; Brecher and Reisman, *op. cit.*, p. 95.

[9] A. E. Safarian and E. B. Carty, "Foreign Financing of Canadian Investment in the Post-War Period," *Proceedings of the Business and Economics Section, American Statistical Association*, 1954, pp. 72-79.

foreign financing in Canadian development since World War II has been considerably less than in previous periods of accelerated growth.[10]

IV

In broad outline, therefore, Canada's contemporary situation is that, while dependence on the outside world as a whole is decreasing, dependence on the United States is increasing. Of fundamental importance is the relative decline of Great Britain as a source of capital and as a market, depriving Canada of its historic counterpoise to the weight of the United States. Current concern over the relations of Canada and the United States reflect the absence of this traditional balance. It is of course clear that in many respects Canada stands to gain from closer economic integration with the United States. The inflow of United States capital, accompanied as it is by transfers of technology, entrepreneurship, and managerial skills, cannot but contribute substantially to rapid growth in Canada. Rising living standards in Canada are but the obverse of the much-criticized dependence on the United States. Nevertheless, dependence has its negative as well as its positive aspects. The character and direction of economic development are as valid matters for concern as the rate, though less easily expressed in simple percentages. Basic to an understanding of the contemporary situation is an appreciation of the qualitative impact of the United States on Canadian growth. The influence of the United States has operated to accelerate the rate of growth of total output in Canada; but it has also served to channel that growth in particular directions.

At the risk of some oversimplification it can be said that the influence of the United States upon the character of Canadian development is in the direction of perpetuating Canada's traditional status as a staple-producing economy. This effect is felt in the impact of United States capital investment in Canada, in the dominant importance of the United States as a market for Canadian exports, and in the prominent role played in the Canadian economy by firms controlled by the United States. Although Canada's over-all dependence on outside financing has been decreasing, in particular sectors of the

[10] Brecher and Reisman estimate that the net use of foreign resources by Canada was about 25 per cent in 1926-1930 and probably larger in 1900-1913. *Op. cit.*, p. 97.

economy dependence on United States investment has been very great. Investment in agriculture, housing, utilities, institutional services, and government is financed predominantly by Canadians. But in manufacturing and in the extractive industries foreign investment has contributed a large, and sometimes the largest, share of the capital required. The book value of total investment in Canadian industry increased by approximately $17.4 billion in the period 1926-1954; more than one-third of this increase represented nonresident investment, and almost all of this one-third came from the United States. In mining and smelting, nonresident financing contributed 65 per cent of total capital expansion in this period, while in manufacturing (which, by the Dominion Bureau of Statistics classification, includes petroleum refining, exploration, and development) the proportion was over 50 per cent.[11] Between 1946 and 1953 approximately one-half of Canada's net capital imports from the United States went into petroleum development; total United States investment in the Canadian petroleum industry reached $1,144 million at the end of 1953, as compared with only $177 million at the end of 1945.[12] By the end of 1953, 56 per cent of the capital employed in Canadian mining, smelting, and petroleum exploration and development companies was nonresident owned, as compared with 39 per cent in 1948 and 36 per cent in 1926.[13]

The impact of United States capital on Canada has therefore been selective. Some has gone into secondary manufacturing; the automobile and rubber industries, to cite only two examples, are dominated by subsidiaries of United States corporations. The greater part of the capital inflow, however, has concentrated in the primary producing sector, particularly nonferrous metals, wood products, and petroleum. The influence of the United States as a market for Canadian exports reinforces this tendency, encouraging development in areas that complement the economy of the United States and discouraging development in areas that are competitive. Of Canada's total exports in 1955, 59.8 per cent were sold to the United States. Of these exports wood, wood products, and paper made up 47.5 per cent, and nonferrous metals and their products about 17 per cent. Developments since 1955 have strengthened this tendency: the Quebec-Labrador iron ore deposits are being exploited to serve the United

[11] *Ibid.*, pp. 98-99.   [12] *Canada Year Book, 1955*, p. 1178.
[13] *Ibid.*, *1956*, p. 1094.

States steel industry; petroleum and natural gas in the prairie provinces must find markets in the United States if their development is not to be seriously retarded. The selective influences of the United States market and of United States investment work in the same direction: capital inflows from the United States since World War II have been heavily concentrated in areas of the economy that contribute directly to exports to the United States. Approximately 70 per cent of the total inflow of direct capital investment from the United States in the period 1946-1955 went into the petroleum, mining, and pulp and paper industries.[14] A similar pattern is evident in the distribution of United States ownership and control in the Canadian economy. While total nonresident ownership of Canadian industry declined from 37 per cent in 1926 to 32 per cent in 1954, the share of the United States increased from 19 per cent to 25 per cent over the same period.[15] In manufacturing and mining, nonresident ownership increased from 42 per cent in 1948 to 51 per cent in 1954, most of the increase representing direct investment by United States companies. According to the definition of control used by the Dominion Bureau of Statistics, at the end of 1955 some 4,957 Canadian enterprises were controlled by non-Canadian interests. Of these, 3,797 were controlled in the United States. In the Canadian petroleum industry the proportion of nonresident control (in terms of capital invested) is 95 per cent; in mining, smelting, and refining, 75 per cent; and in manufacturing, 57 per cent. United States interests account for the bulk of nonresident control in each case.[16]

In its broad outlines the situation is a simple one: United States capital flows into Canada principally to accelerate development in sectors that will serve the United States market. Since the United States is already a highly industrialized economy with a very productive agricultural sector, the market demand that it exerts on Canada is predominantly a demand for industrial raw materials. The rate of economic development in Canada depends largely upon exploiting such demand. The influence of the United States is therefore such as to encourage the development of the Canadian economy along lines complementary to the economy of the United States. This casts Canada, in its relations with the United States, in the role of a supplier of unmanufactured or semimanufactured products. The

[14] Brecher and Reisman, *op. cit.,* p. 95.
[15] *Ibid.,* p. 99.   [16] *Ibid.,* pp. 285-287.

structure of the United States tariff reflects and reinforces the pressure already exerted by the pattern of United States demand and by the movement into Canada of United States labor, capital, and entrepreneurship.

This structural relationship between the two economies is fundamental. Clearly it is not the kind of thing that short-range government policies can do much to change. The development of a national economy does not take place *in vacuo*, but rather in a conjuncture of opportunities and obstacles. Development depends upon exploiting the opportunities and overcoming the obstacles. The proximity of the United States economy, as a market and as a source of investment capital in particular, structures this environment of opportunities and obstacles in such a way that the Canadian economy tends to develop in the direction of primary production for the United States market.

To many Canadians such a trend, for political as well as economic reasons, appears undesirable. They would prefer to see more diversification of the economy and less dependence on external markets. In particular, they would prefer a situation in which control over the future direction of growth of the Canadian economy rested more in the hands of Canadians and less in the hands of foreigners, however convenient the support and assistance of those foreigners may be. The attitude itself is understandable; the suggested policies to which it gives rise, however, are of questionable effectiveness and rarely show an appreciation of the real costs of nationalism.[17]

The dilemma facing Canada at the moment is that policies adopted to modify the character and direction of Canadian economic growth involve imposing restrictions upon the transfer to Canada of capital and entrepreneurship from the United States, upon the operations of United States-controlled corporations in Canada, and upon the marketing of Canadian exports. Such policies necessarily entail the possibility, indeed the probability, of a retardation of the rate of economic growth in Canada. The problem, therefore, is to devise policies that will have a maximum effect on modifying the character of development in directions more congenial to Canadian sentiment, and at the same time will have a minimum effect on retarding the rate of

[17] Harry G. Johnson, "Canada's Economic Prospects," *Canadian Journal of Economics and Political Science*, XXIV (1958), 104-110; Jacob Viner, "The Gordon Commission Report," *Queen's Quarterly*, LXIV (1957), 305-325.

growth. This problem is, of course, by no means unique to Canada, and it is not new. Similar dilemmas are typical of all exposed and relatively less-developed countries operating within the orbit of a major industrial economy. Furthermore, they have been encountered at earlier periods in Canadian economic history.

The analytical dissection of the problem as it affects particular sectors of the Canadian economy, and the appraisal of some of the policies that have been suggested to grapple with it, are the tasks of the papers which follow in this volume. It seems worthwhile at this point to review briefly Canada's past experience in attempting to modify the character of economic development in the face of countervailing pressure from the United States. In the remainder of this paper, therefore, we shall consider relevant phases in the development of four of Canada's major industries, each of which has involved the exploitation of important Canadian natural resources, and each of which has been influenced decisively by United States capital and by the United States market. These four are, in order, pulp and paper, nickel, petroleum, and natural gas.

v

The pulp and paper industry is the classic example of the successful exercise of government power to attract to Canada manufacturing industries utilizing Canadian raw materials.[18] The primary instrument of policy was the export tariff, manipulated in such a way as to induce pulp and paper mills to migrate toward the source of their raw materials. Essential to the success of this policy, however, was a particular conjuncture of circumstances: the rapidly growing demand for newsprint in the United States; the depletion of United States domestic supplies of pulpwood, with consequent rising costs; the availability in Canada of cheap and plentiful supplies, not only of pulpwood, but also of hydroelectricity; and the fact that almost all of Canada's pulpwood resources were controlled by Canadian provincial governments, never having been alienated into private ownership.

United States imports of Canadian pulpwood began to rise sharply in the last decades of the nineteenth century, reflecting the increasing

[18] Material on the pulp and paper industry has been drawn predominantly from John A. Guthrie, *The Newsprint Paper Industry, An Economic Analysis* (Cambridge, Mass., 1941); but see also W. T. Easterbrook and Hugh G. J. Aitken, *Canadian Economic History* (Toronto, 1956), pp. 538-546.

scarcity of pulpwood in the United States and lower costs of production in Canada. Had no action been taken by the Canadian provincial governments to exploit this situation, the sole result of the increase in demand might well have been an increase in exports of unmanufactured pulpwood, destined to be processed into newsprint and other papers in mills located in the United States. Other possibilities, however, were implicit in the situation. The United States demand for newsprint was highly inelastic: prices could be raised without serious danger of a decline in quantities sold. Furthermore, Canada was in the position of a partial, if not complete, monopolist: there was at that time no other large source of supply upon which United States consumers could conveniently draw. The advantage in bargaining power clearly lay with Canadian suppliers. This advantage could have been used to demand higher prices for pulpwood exports. It was used instead to compel movement of the newsprint manufacturing processes to Canada.

The initiative was taken by Canadian provincial governments, since they, and not the Dominion government, controlled the forest resources. In 1891 British Columbia prohibited the export of timber cut on Crown lands; Ontario adopted a similar prohibition in 1902; meanwhile, Quebec in 1900 imposed what was in effect an export duty on pulpwood by reducing the fee on timber cut on Crown lands by approximately one-third provided that the wood was manufactured into newsprint in Canada. Export duties on pulpwood were enacted by the Dominion government in 1897.

The ultimate objective was to compel the migration of the manufacturing processes to Canada, thus securing the benefit of larger payrolls, greater taxable capacity, and more valuable exports. Retaliation by the United States government was the principal hazard, but even this was severely limited by the nature of demand and supply conditions. In 1909 the United States Congress offered to reduce the tariff on the lowest grade of paper imports if the Canadian provinces would remove all restrictions on pulpwood exports. When the offer was ignored, a retaliatory duty of $2.00 per ton was imposed on Canadian paper. American newspaper publishers, however, bore the real burden of this tariff in the form of higher newsprint prices, and were in a position to exert powerful pressure on Congress to repeal the duty. Free entry for Canadian newsprint was offered in the proposed reciprocity agreement of 1911, which was rejected by the Canadian electorate. The collapse of all attempts at retaliation by the United States was marked by the passage of the Underwood Tariff of 1913, which provided for the free admission of newsprint paper valued at not more than 2½ cents per pound. Since that time Canadian newsprint has entered the United States market free of duty.[19]

The manufacture of pulp and paper is today Canada's leading industry, no matter what criterion is used, and accounts for some 47 per cent by value of all Canadian exports to the United States. Basic to the remarkable growth of the industry has been free entry of its product into the United States market, and, as a consequence, the migration of newsprint mills to Canada to exploit the locational advantages of proximity to the raw material and to the cheap hydroelectricity of the Canadian Shield. That the successful export strategy of Canadian governments contributed significantly to the establishment and development of the industry in Canada cannot be doubted. The peculiar circumstances of the case, however, must be emphasized: the semimonopolistic position of Canadian suppliers; the low elasticity of demand of United States consumers; and the fundamental locational pull of cheap power and raw materials. In the absence of these highly advantageous circumstances, the strategy would not have been effective. The example of the newsprint industry gives no guarantee of success for a general application of similar policies.

VI

In the case of the nickel industry the basic objective of Canadian policy was the same: to attract the later stages of production (in this case refining) to Canada.[20] The difficulties were, however, much greater. The nickel-copper ore deposits of the Sudbury basin in northern Ontario were discovered in 1883. Intensive exploitation began about 1890 with the development of nickel-steel alloys for armor plate. The rapid growth of the Sudbury basin as a major

[19] It is alleged, however, that the specifications of the United States tariff are such as to make it unprofitable for Canadian firms to produce and export to the United States newsprint of a quality higher than that currently sold, even though such a higher-grade product could be produced by Canadian mills without large increases in cost. Similarly, the United States tariff bars Canadian firms from competing in the American market for high-grade coated papers.

[20] The account which follows is based upon O. W. Main, *The Canadian Nickel Industry: A Study in Market Control and Public Policy*, Canadian Studies in Economics, No. 4 (Toronto, 1955).

source of nickel ore and nickel concentrate resulted from the ability of the Orford Company, which processed Canadian nickel at refineries in the United States, to secure control of the United States market and to break into the European market in competition with the major French producer, Le Nickel. In 1902 Canada supplied 45 per cent of the world market for nickel ore and matte; by 1913 the proportion had risen to 70 per cent. In the latter year Canadian nickel ore supplied 60 per cent of the European market and 100 per cent of the American.

The basis for the dominance of the industry by companies operating in Canada was the large size of the deposits, which made possible significant economies of scale, and relatively low costs of transportation to the major centers of consumption. Canada was in a position to force marginal producers out of existence and to prevent new sources of supply from developing. In the initial period of development the dominant firm operating in the Sudbury basin was the Canadian Copper Company, an enterprise controlled by United States capital which was by far the most powerful and at times the only producer in the area. Canadian Copper operated smelters in the Sudbury basin and exported nickel matte to the Orford Company's refineries in Ohio. The Orford Company, in turn, sold refined nickel on exclusive contract to the U. S. Navy Department and to the leading firms in the United States steel industry. The interrelationships between the various interests involved were close from the beginning. The formation of the International Nickel Company in 1902 marked their consolidation into a single concern. As a holding company, International Nickel took over the properties formerly owned by Canadian Copper in Sudbury and the Orford refineries in Cleveland. Ultimate control rested in the hands of the financial group behind the United States Steel Corporation, under the leadership of J. P. Morgan.

Neither International Nickel nor its predecessors were ever free from the threat of competition, potential or actual. Defenses against encroachments upon its monopoly position were, however, formidable: long-term contracts with the major consumers; financial connections with J. P. Morgan & Co., who were in a position to prevent public financing of possible competitors; and, when necessary, aggressive price warfare. No less dangerous to the position of the enterprise, however, was the threat of hostile public opinion and unfavorable political action in Canada. In the first place, the firm was a monopoly and for that reason vulnerable to criticism. Secondly, though exploiting a Canadian resource, it was controlled by United States capital. And thirdly, the company steadfastly refused to refine its nickel in Canada, insisting that it was economically necessary for its survival to do the refining in the United States. During the entire period to 1915, when the first Canadian nickel refinery was established at Port Colborne, International Nickel and its predecessor, Canadian Copper, were functioning in a hostile political and social environment under the imminent danger of punitive legislative action and possibly expropriation.

The difficult position of the company became clear as early as 1890. In January of that year a spokesman for Canadian Copper appeared before a committee of the United States Senate to plead for the retention of the import duty on refined nickel, but the abolition of all duties on nickel ore and matte. Such an adjustment of the tariff would enable the company to establish a refinery in the United States and gain a monopoly of the United States market. The McKinley tariff of 1890 embodied the desired provisions: nickel ore and matte were admitted free, while a duty of 10 cents a pound was imposed on refined nickel. This gave the Sudbury mines exclusive possession of the United States market, as other sources of supply (in particular New Caledonia) could not ship ore at competitive prices. The monopoly position of Canadian Copper in the United States now seemed secure. But its position in Canada was seriously jeopardized, for the Canadian federal government and the provincial government of Ontario were alike determined that a nickel refinery should be built in Canada as the foundation for a Canadian nickel-steel industry. On the one hand it was alleged that Canadian Copper had received its charter on the promise that the ore would be refined in Canada. On the other the company asserted that, if the refining were done in Canada, it would be driven out of the United States market by competitors refining in that country and by an increase in the tariff on refined nickel. The impasse was clear: if the company refined in the United States, it jeopardized its position in Canada; if it refined in Canada, it might lose its monopoly in the United States.

Unfavorable public opinion in Canada, sedulously encouraged by would-be competitors, found its reflection in unfavorable legislation. A rival syndicate in 1896 appealed to the Canadian government to impose an export duty on nickel ore and matte, arguing that the refining of the ore in Canada was not only economically possible but also a national necessity. Canadian Copper presented the usual arguments in defense: it had no refining process of its own, but had to rely on the Orford Company in the United States; the Orford process required cheap chemicals, skilled labor, and a market for by-products, and these were not available in Canada.[21] The Canadian Parliament, accurately reflecting nationalistic sentiment in Canada, responded in 1897 by imposing an export duty of 10 cents a pound on nickel "contained in matte, or in the ore, or in any crude or partially manufactured state"—a step precisely analogous, it may be noted, to the export duties on pulpwood enacted at the same time. The export duties on nickel, however, were to be imposed only when proclaimed by the Governor in Council. Strong opposition from local landowners in the Sudbury area and from Canadian Copper, which threatened to close down entirely, prevented the necessary Order in Council from being issued at that time. The duty remained on the statute books as an ever-present threat, but action by the Dominion government was effectively blocked for the time being.

The initiative in the campaign against Canadian Copper now passed to the provincial government of Ontario. Already Ontario had successfully compelled the movement of the sawn lumber industry from Michigan to Ontario by prohibiting the cutting of pine on Crown lands unless the logs were manufactured into sawn lumber in Canada. Might not a similar strategy move the refining of nickel to Ontario? In 1899 the provincial government issued an Order in Council emphasizing the desirability of encouraging the entry of British capital into the Sudbury basin, of putting into effect the export duties on nickel ore and matte earlier approved by the Dominion Parliament, and of insuring that in future all grants of mining lands should require that the ore be refined within the province. In December of that year a formal request was made to the Dominion government to impose the export duties. When this produced no result, the Ontario government took independent action to amend the Mines Act of 1891 by imposing a tax on unrefined copper and nickel ores. Despite strong opposition from Canadian Copper and allied

---

[21] At the same time, it may be noted, Canadian Copper was arguing before the United States Congress that an import duty on nickel ore would compel a shift of refining to England. See Main, *op. cit.*, pp. 40-41.

mining interests, the Act was passed. It provided that every person carrying on the business of mining in the province should pay a license fee based on the gross quantity of ore mined. If the ores were treated in Canada to yield fine metal, the fees would be refunded. The Act was to come into force upon proclamation by the Lieutenant Governor.

In the face of this threat the ability and resourcefulness of Canadian Copper and its allies in the United States were once again demonstrated. The Act was passed, but it was never proclaimed. As a gesture toward meeting the wishes of the provincial government, Canadian Copper erected in Canada a Bessemer smelting plant; this produced, not refined nickel, but a considerably richer matte. More significantly, the Orford Company, obdurate in its determination not to refine in Canada, began stock-piling nickel matte and developing alternative sources of nickel ore. The threat to close down nickel mining in Canada was not wholly a bluff. The step that definitely blocked government action for the time being was the formation of the International Nickel Company in 1902. The new concern, possessing large financial resources, closely linked to the United States Steel Corporation, and backed by the influence and prestige of J. P. Morgan, was clearly in a position to dominate the United States nickel market without relying on Canadian ore and to prevent the establishment of a nickel-steel industry in Canada. Deprived of access to the United States market, the Sudbury area would certainly have been forced to close down. Despite the fact, therefore, that both political parties, before the election of June, 1902, had pledged themselves to secure the refining of mineral products in Ontario, nothing in fact was done to impose the export duties or the license fees on unrefined nickel.

The impasse continued until World War I. In the prewar period International Nickel expanded its refining capacity in the United States to meet the rising demand for armaments; in 1913 it built a new refinery in New Jersey—a step which could hardly have alienated Canadian opinion more effectively if it had been planned for that purpose. No move was made to establish a refinery in Canada, despite the fact that the product could have been exported to Europe, if not to the United States. The climate of public opinion in Canada remained extremely hostile, the company's chief defense being repetitions of the argument that no refining process suitable to the Canadian environment had yet been discovered. This claim no longer carried conviction. Meanwhile a new element entered the controversy in support of Canadian nationalism: the strategic importance of nickel in time of war. Increasingly it came to be felt that national and imperial security required access to refined nickel within the Empire. The fact that International Nickel was under United States control was felt to be a potential danger. With the outbreak of war in 1914 this issue became urgent. It was essential on the one hand to maintain the flow of refined metal to Britain, and on the other to prevent its shipment to Germany. Canada, however, had no means of controlling the final destination of refined nickel exported from the United States, nor of refining nickel independently. Accusations that International Nickel was under German influence and was in fact shipping nickel to Germay became common, and agitation grew to compel the government to prohibit the export of unrefined nickel, to take over the operation of the nickel mines, and to establish a government-owned refinery in Canada. International Nickel refused to modify its policies. Pressure from the Imperial Munitions Board led both the Dominion and Ontario governments to appoint commissions of inquiry, and the possibility of a government subsidy to a competitor of International was seriously discussed. Allegations that the German submarine *Deutschland* had actually carried two cargoes of Canadian nickel from the United States to Germany provided the final dramatic touch. Under direct pressure from Dominion and provincial governments, the fear of expropriation, and an aroused public opinion, International Nickel finally consented to construct a nickel refinery in Canada. The site chosen was Port Colborne, Ontario, and the refinery was completed in July, 1918.

The processes underlying this tangled story have been well summarized by Professor Main. In the period up to 1902 government policy to compel refining in Canada was frustrated by the retaliatory power of the United States and the strategic position of the Canadian Copper-Orford alliance. "The inability of a nationalistic sentiment to find effective instruments of control for export industries, as the tariff had been for home industries, strengthened the development of industries in the industrial nations at the expense of the fringe areas."[22] The United States tariff, structured in favor of raw material imports, kept the refining industry located close to the market.

[22] *Ibid.*, p. 59.

The pull of raw materials in Canada was insufficient to offset the pull of the market in the United States when that market was protected by an appropriate tariff. The absence within the industry of serious competitors who might have been more amenable to Canadian pressure in the hope of securing an advantage over the dominant firm aggravated the difficulties. The situation might well have continued indefinitely had not war intervened. In time of peace, because of the strength of International Nickel, the generally laissez-faire philosophy of Canadian governments, and the danger of seriously retarding the development of the Sudbury area, sufficient pressure could not be mobilized to induce the desired change in corporate policy. Only the emergencies of war, implying the necessity for control over a vital war material and backed by the threat of expropriation, made the pressure finally effective.[23]

Policies that achieved success in newsprint proved ineffective for nickel. The effectiveness of export duties as a means of attracting industry depended upon two principal factors: (1) the degree of monopoly enjoyed by Canada in the market for her exports and (2) the locational pull of Canadian resources as compared with the locational pull of the United States market. In nickel Canada had massive advantages in terms of production and transfer costs; but other sources of supply, in particular New Caledonia, were always available to consumers as a defense. Ample supplies of nickel ore did not in themselves constitute an overriding attractive force in determining the location of the refining process. Not until the development of electrolytic refining after World War I did the locational advantages of refining in Canada become decisive, the pull of cheap hydroelectric power reinforcing the pull of the Sudbury ores.

VII

The petroleum and natural gas industries are of recent development in Canada, although small oil deposits of local importance in southern Ontario and the foothills of the Rocky Mountains were exploited during the late nineteenth and early twentieth centuries. Public policy toward the industry has not yet finally crystallized. It is already apparent, however, that the problems involved in insuring that the industry contributes in the most desirable way to Canadian

[23] *Ibid.*, pp. 85-89.

development are significantly different from those encountered, for example, in the forest products and nickel industries. Canadian resources of petroleum are directly competitive with those of the United States. There are, therefore, no prospects of attaining a position of monopoly in this product; on the contrary, a serious problem exists of securing stable access to the United States market. On the other hand, exploitation of Canada's resources of natural gas promises to contribute very substantially to the basic energy resources for Canadian manufacturing. There is, therefore, a problem of insuring that the long-term energy requirements of the Canadian economy are adequately provided for, and that the industry does not become too dependent on United States outlets. Access to the United States market is the primary problem for petroleum; restricting exports to the United States in the interests of the manufacturing complex of central Canada is the primary problem for natural gas. Public policy has differed considerably between the two products.

The Canadian oil industry antedates that of the United States. The first producing oil well in North America was drilled at Black Creek in southern Ontario in 1858, one year before the famous Drake well in Pennsylvania. For many years, however, the industry in Canada appeared to have no very promising future. The southern Ontario wells reached their peak output in 1890 and declined thereafter, remaining significant only as a local source of natural gas. Meanwhile in the western provinces oil and natural gas resources were discovered in the foothills of the Rockies, at Medicine Hat in 1890 and at Turner Valley, near Calgary, in 1914. These fields were of minor importance and gave little encouragement for further exploration. Until the end of the World War II, however, they were, with the remote Norman Wells field on the Mackenzie River, the only producing areas in Canada.

During World War II the rate of exploration for oil in western Canada increased considerably. Prospects for major advances depended upon the discovery of oil-bearing formations in the plains area outside the foothill belt. The major break-through occurred with the opening up of the Leduc field in Alberta by Imperial Oil, a United States controlled company, in 1946. With this discovery the Canadian oil industry entered a period of rapid expansion which is still continuing—an expansion, be it noted, largely stimulated and supported by the influx of United States capital, entrepreneurship, and technology. Crude petroleum production in Alberta, which in 1944 had been only 8.7 million barrels, rose by 1954 to 87.7 million; for Canada as a whole the corresponding figures were 10 million and 96 million.[24]

By the end of 1952 it was apparent that the further development of the Canadian oil industry depended less upon the discovery of additional reserves than upon access to markets. Local demand in the prairie provinces, with only 18 per cent of Canada's population, was too small to absorb more than a fraction of the potential output. Growth hinged upon the construction of transportation facilities to carry the crude oil to refineries in areas closer to the centers of population and industry—specifically in central Canada and on the Pacific coast. It was realized that in each of these markets Canadian crude would have to meet the competition not only of United States oil but also of imported supplies arriving by tanker from Venezuela and the Middle East. Pipelines provided the only possible solution to the problem. Techniques for transmitting oil and gas over long distances by pipeline had been perfected in the United States during World War II. Further development of the Canadian oil industry depended upon applying these techniques in Canada.

The market in central Canada was the first to be opened up. Late in 1950 the Interprovincial pipeline was built from Edmonton, Alberta, to Superior, Wisconsin, making it possible to transport oil from the Alberta fields to the refinery operated by Imperial Oil at Sarnia, Ontario, the oil going by pipeline to Superior and then by lake tanker from Superior to Sarnia. The effects of its completion were shown in a 68 per cent increase in Alberta's production of crude oil between 1950 and 1951. The capacity of this pipeline soon proved inadequate, and in 1953 an extension was completed from Superior across the Straits of Mackinac and the Michigan peninsula and thence directly to Sarnia. Construction was also begun on a pipeline to carry refined petroleum products from Sarnia to London, Hamilton, and Toronto.

Construction of the Interprovincial pipeline enabled the Canadian oil industry to reach the largest market then available in Canada. Access to this market, too, did not depend on United States tariff policy—a consideration which carried considerable weight. Before the construction of the pipeline, southern Ontario had been supplied

[24] *Canada Year Book, 1952-53*, p. 544; *Ibid., 1956*, p. 530.

with oil from fields in Illinois, Kansas, and Oklahoma. With the completion of the pipeline, purchases of American oil began to decrease, as oil from the western prairies edged Mid-Continental oil out of the Ontario market.

On the Pacific coast there existed a potential market for oil at least as large as that in central Canada. The Pacific Northwest (Oregon, Washington, and British Columbia) is an area deficient in fuels, as is Ontario. Imports from California and to some extent from Venezuela and the Middle East normally provide the necessary supplies. Known oil reserves in California, however, were dwindling, and there seemed a reasonable prospect that Alberta crude could take over some of the market, provided that ocean tanker freight rates did not decline drastically. Accordingly, construction of the Transmountain pipeline from Edmonton to Vancouver was begun in 1952 and completed late in 1953. It was appreciated at the time that the demand in British Columbia alone was inadequate to justify the very large investment involved. Only if the market in Oregon and Washington could be tapped was the project feasible. This meant that the success of the Transmountain pipeline, and of the Alberta oil fields that fed it, depended on United States import policy. This question did not arise in connection with the eastern pipeline to central Canada; it was of crucial importance for the pipeline to the Pacific coast.

Construction of these two pipelines provided an outlet for 600,-000 barrels of oil daily from western Canada, if markets were available for that quantity. This was a figure considerably in excess of the actual output of Canadian wells at that time. The problem to be faced in the future was no longer one of inadequate transport facilities, nor one of production, but a problem of pricing and markets. Oil from western Canada was now in competition with oil from the United States, from the Middle East, and from Venezuela. Could it meet this competition successfully?

The market on the Pacific coast initially proved a serious disappointment. It is sometimes forgotten that oil can be moved by ocean tanker at costs per mile considerably less than by pipeline. Low tanker rates in 1953 meant that oil from the Middle East could undersell Alberta oil in the Pacific Northwest. In these circumstances most of the crude oil was shipped to central Canada for refining. The Ontario market, however, was approaching saturation by the end of

1953. Further development depended upon securing new markets. Two major possibilities were open: first, to invade the American Midwestern market by constructing refineries in Wisconsin and Michigan; and secondly, to seek market outlets in the province of Quebec. Neither of these possibilities appeared very promising. Attempts to invade the American market would have to surmount the American tariff of 10.5 cents a barrel on light crude oil and would entail substantial cuts in the well-head price in Canada. The Montreal market was normally supplied by Venezuelan oil, shipped by tanker to Portland, Maine, and thence by pipeline to Montreal. In view of the abundance of oil in world markets at that time and the low level of tanker freights, it seemed improbable that western Canadian oil could invade the Montreal market in competition with Venezuelan imports without a very substantial cut in price and well-head receipts.

By the end of 1953, therefore, the Canadian oil industry had reached the end of its first stage of spectacular expansion. Exploration and development continued apace, but distribution and marketing were the primary problems. The phase during which it had been hoped that whole regional markets might be captured had passed; development hinged upon the secular increase of demand within Canada, and the much more problematic prospects of increasing sales to the United States. By the end of 1954, the Canadian oil industry was supplying practically all crude oil requirements in Canada between Vancouver and Toronto. In that year British Columbia turned entirely to Canadian crude, while Ontario reduced its imports to one-fifth of its requirements.

Government policy toward the oil industry has been confined to provincial legislation controlling leases and conservation policy. No impediment has been placed in the way of pipeline construction, nor has any attempt been made to restrict access to the United States market. The issue has, in fact, been precisely the opposite: to facilitate access to the United States and thereby accelerate the development of crude oil resources in Canada. It seems clear that further rapid growth of the Canadian oil industry requires market outlets in the United States. In aggregate terms the Canadian economy is already approaching self-sufficiency in oil. The industry must either gear its expansion to the growth of Canadian domestic demand (which would mean a marked retardation of the past rate of development) or it must export to the United States. In helping the industry gain access to the United States, however, the Canadian government operates under serious handicaps. There is no vestige in this industry of the monopolistic position enjoyed in pulpwood and nickel. United States domestic oil producers have demonstrated their determination to retain a preferred position in their home market: their political influence has been made plain by the so-called voluntary restriction of crude imports. The public justification for these import restrictions runs in terms of the need to maintain the domestic rate of exploration for oil and avoid undue dependence on reserves outside the political and strategic control of the United States. This argument is unconvincing: if it is desirable to protect the oil reserves of the United States, rational policy would suggest the encouragement of imports while imports are available, and the conservation of domestic reserves for use in future emergency. As applied to Canada the logic is particularly questionable, for Canadian oil reserves are located within the United States defense perimeter and are properly to be considered, as far as defense strategy is concerned, as available to the United States in all circumstances. Actually the argument from defense seems no more than a smoke screen. Restrictions on oil imports are a means of maintaining domestic oil prices in a period of slackening demand. They serve the same price-maintenance function as do most conservation statutes and are equivalent to an increase in the tariff.[25] There seems little that Canada can do, however, to alter the situation, and it appears probable that access to the United States market will remain, within the foreseeable future, an unreliable foundation for Canadian oil development. Any softening of oil prices in the United States will probably lead to import restrictions of some

[25] Voluntary import quotas as currently in force in the United States have not yet seriously retarded the growth of the Canadian oil industry, principally because import from Canada (and Venezuela) are given preferred treatment over Middle Eastern supplies. Nevertheless, it seems highly probable that such import quotas will in future set a ceiling on sales of Canadian crude in the United States. American companies in western Canada are in any case unlikely to make the price cuts necessary for a successful invasion of the United States market by Canadian oil since such action would adversely affect the profitability of United States wells and probably lead to political pressure for more stringent import controls. This is one area in which the interests of United States-controlled companies operating in Canada may clearly diverge from the Canadian national interest. Opinions as to the seriousness of such a divergence of interest will vary according to one's views of proper conservation policy for Canadian oil. It is not uncommon to find United States-controlled corporations criticized both for retarding the development of Canadian resources and for depleting those resources too quickly. On the prospects for Canadian oil exports, see John Davis, *Canadian Energy Prospects* (Ottawa, 1957), pp. 125-171.

sort. The fact that some of the leading United States oil companies have extensive investments in oil properties and refineries outside the United States affords greater hope for a gradual relaxation of policy than does any pressure that Canada can apply.

VIII

United States policy has been no less decisive in the case of natural gas, though the problems are very different. On the supply side, petroleum and natural gas are joint products; retardation of the development of petroleum reserves influences the supply of natural gas and vice versa. On the demand side, however, natural gas has a particular importance as a cheap and convenient source of industrial heat, whereas the demand for petroleum is largely a demand for motive power. When it is recalled that the industrial complex of central Canada has always heretofore depended on imports of United States coal for its heat resources, the national importance of the natural gas industry becomes clear. Government policy in Canada has in fact been directed largely toward insuring that the industrial needs of central Canada have priority over exports to the United States.

Pipeline construction has been the focus of this policy. In 1937 the government of Alberta announced that no exports of gas from the province would be permitted until reserves had been proved adequate to provide a thirty-year supply for the province and to meet the prior needs of the Dominion. In 1951 the provincial Conservation Board agreed that the first of these two conditions had been met, and in that year the provincial government authorized the export of gas to supply the refinery of the Anaconda Copper Company at Butte, Montana.[26] Shortly thereafter permission was given to the Westcoast Transmission Company to build a pipeline from the Peace River area to Vancouver and thence to Portland and Seattle. Construction of this pipeline, however, was contingent upon securing per-

[26] This contract has been severely criticized in Canada. The gas was supplied by a Canadian subsidiary of the Montana Power Company, which was permitted to charge its parent company a price substantially lower than would have prevailed under "arm's-length" competitive bargaining. Anaconda's smelter at Butte was thus enabled to secure Canadian gas at a cost between one-half and one-third less than it would otherwise have had to pay for energy in the form of coal or residual oil; the price received at the well-head in Alberta was reduced correspondingly. See Davis, *op. cit.*, pp. 166-167.

mission for the U. S. Federal Power Commission to build the extension in the United States, Canadian demand in the area being insufficient to justify the investment. In June, 1954, this permission was refused, largely because of the opposition of an American company, the Northwest Pipe Line Corporation, which proposed to serve the Pacific Northwest with gas from New Mexico. It became clear that Canadian gas would be permitted to enter the United States only on terms acceptable to United States producers and pipe-line companies. An agreement was worked out in December, 1954, by which the Canadian company agreed to deliver gas to the Northwest Pipe Line Corporation at the United States border for distribution by the American company (which became part-owner of the Westcoast project). Canadian gas from the Peace River area will before long serve the whole Pacific Northwest, as the promoters of the Westcoast Transmission Company originally intended. But it will do so at prices considerably less remunerative to the Canadian producer than would have obtained had the Federal Power Commission interpreted the American public interest more broadly. Canadian gas wells are the logical, indeed the only adequate, source of supply for the region. Except as a means of protecting the interests of American gas producers and pipe line companies, it is hard to see any reasonable justification for refusing the original Canadian application.[27]

Further permits for the export of gas from Alberta to the United States would probably have followed if the Dominion government had not intervened. In March, 1953, the Minister of Trade and Commerce announced that the export policy applied since 1907 to electric power would in future be applied to natural gas also, and that in consequence all further exports of gas from Canada would be prohibited until such time as the government was convinced that there could be no economic use, present or future, for that gas in Canada. This meant in practice that gas from the western prairies would have to be piped to central Canada before the government would sanction exports. It later emerged that the government would

[27] *Ibid.*, pp. 165-166. See also Freeman Lincoln, "Frank McMahon's Pipe Dream," *Fortune*, Jan., 1958, pp. 146 ff. The contract between the Pacific Northwest Pipe Line Company and the Westcoast Transmission Company included the unusual provision that the border price for gas should remain fixed for the full twenty-year period of the contract—a striking indication of the weak bargaining power of the Canadian interests. The ability of American regulatory agencies to influence Canadian economic policy is a topic that would repay further investigation.

approve the construction of a gas pipe line to central Canada only on condition that it did not pass through the United States. The objectives of the policy were two: first, to insure that Canadian industries in Ontario, a fuel-deficient region, should have priority in securing gas from western Canada; and second, to insure that this vital artery, when built, should be entirely within Canadian control and not subject to interruption under any circumstances by the United States.

The motives behind the policy were clear; to implement it proved difficult. Could private business interests raise the necessary capital to build a pipe line which met the government's requirements? This capital, whether raised by the sale of stock or by the subscriptions of gas-producing companies, would necessarily be in large part American in origin, for it was highly improbable that a sufficient amount could be raised entirely from Canadian sources. The issue came down to this: could United States capital be induced to finance the construction of a gas pipe line from Alberta to Ontario entirely through Canadian territory, when a much preferable route (from a commercial point of view) was available running in part through the United States?

The analogies with government railroad policy in the 1870's and 1880's were clear. At that time the Dominion government had insisted that Canada's first transcontinental railroad should be built north of the Great Lakes, entirely through Canadian territory; this stipulation had made necessary large government subsidies in the form of cash and land grants. In the case of the gas pipe line too, an all-Canadian route was regarded as indispensable.[28] The instrument of government policy in this instance was Trans-Canada Pipe Lines, Limited, a private corporation originally chartered by Parliament in 1951. At that time it was a wholly owned subsidiary of Canadian Delhi Oil, Limited, a company controlled by Clint Murchison, the well-known American oil and gas entrepreneur. Trans-Canada's original purpose was to construct and operate a gas pipe line from Alberta to Ontario, the route to run north of the Great Lakes

---

[28] There were at least two alternatives: first, to allow gas to be exported to the United States from the Calgary area and recovered in the vicinity of Toronto on an exchange basis; and, second, to allow the gas pipe line to follow the same route as the oil pipe line from Alberta—that is, a route through the United States. Both these possibilities were considered but rejected by the Canadian government. For an explanation of the decision, see the remarks of the Minister of Trade and Commerce in *Hansard*, March 15, 1956.

entirely through Canadian territory. No export of gas to the United States was envisaged, and the statute of incorporation restricted the company to activity within Canada. No government assistance beyond the necessary permits was asked for or contemplated.

Whether such a project could have been successfully financed and carried to completion must remain a matter of opinion, for its feasibility was never put to the test. In 1953 Trans-Canada applied to the Alberta Conservation Board for a permit to export gas from the province to eastern Canada. About the same time, a second company, Western Pipe Lines, Limited, representing Winnipeg interests, also applied for a permit, its stated objectives being to pipe gas to Winnipeg and also, in substantial quantities, to the United States. The provincial government refused both applications on the grounds that neither company met its requirements for financial viability, but suggested that if the two companies were to amalgamate an export license might be granted. The merger took place in early 1954; at that time the Trans-Canada project was broadened to include the export of gas to the United States at Emerson, Manitoba, as well as the construction of the all-Canadian line to Ontario originally proposed.

Up to this point the Dominion government had not formally intervened. It soon became evident, however, that the completion of the Trans-Canada pipe line was likely to be seriously delayed. The financial feasibility of the project depended upon the granting of permission for the import of gas at Emerson by the United States Federal Power Commission. Without this permission Trans-Canada would undoubtedly have great difficulty in raising capital in the United States, and without such capital the project could hardly be carried out. The Company's application to the F.P.C., however, ran into such severe opposition from certain United States gas pipe line companies that favorable action seemed very improbable and quick action unattainable. Meanwhile in Canada there was increasing political and economic pressure for an early start with construction. In these circumstances the Dominion government made its first move to extend direct aid to the Company. Late in 1955 it was announced that the section of the pipe line north of the Great Lakes—the so-called Ontario bridge—would be built by the government through a Crown corporation. The capital required would be provided jointly by the Ontario provincial government and the Dominion government, and on completion the pipe line would be leased to

Trans-Canada on terms which made early purchase by the Company almost certain. This measure of public assistance, it was hoped, would enable the Company to secure the necessary capital to begin construction without awaiting favorable action by the Federal Power Commission.

In the meantime the government found itself exposed to public and parliamentary criticism for its apparent failure to give serious consideration to an alternative proposal emanating from a syndicate headed by Frank McMahon of Calgary, a Canadian, promoter of Pacific Petroleums, Limited and of the Westcoast Transmission Company. McMahon's group offered to build the pipe line without subsidy of any kind, apparently relying on their connections with the New York financial house of Eastman Dillon-Union Securities. The Liberal government, however, declined to be distracted from its policy of support to Trans-Canada. It was pointed out that the McMahon syndicate proposed to export 300 million cubic feet of gas per day to the United States at Emerson, in contrast to the 200 million proposed by Trans-Canada; that McMahon held no signed contracts either at the producing or the distributing end, whereas Trans-Canada not only had such contracts but also held an option for the necessary 34-inch pipe; and that the McMahon offer was never formally submitted to the Cabinet, being contained merely in private and confidential correspondence with the Minister of Trade and Commerce. In the event the McMahon offer was withdrawn.

Having undertaken this large measure of aid to Trans-Canada, however, the government soon found that it had to go further. Even with its liability confined to the prairie section, the Trans-Canada corporation was unable to raise sufficient capital to begin construction by the date specified, essentially because the approval of the Federal Power Commission for exports of gas to the United States had not been secured. The government therefore proposed to lend to Trans-Canada from public funds the sum of $80 million to finance 90 per cent of the cost of building the western section from the Alberta border to Winnipeg.[29] This proposal was submitted to Parliament

[29] By this time substantial ownership shares in Trans-Canada had been purchased by Canadian Gulf Oil, Hudson's Bay Oil and Gas (a subsidiary of the Continental Oil Company), and by the Tennessee Gas Transmission Company, so that the whole enterprise had a definitely American character, representing an alliance of the major United States oil and gas companies operating in western Canada (which were at the same time the largest holders of proven gas reserves in Alberta), and one of the

and aroused considerable controversy. Many felt that the government should have accepted the offer of the McMahon syndicate,
which had the appearance, at least, of being less under the control
of United States interests; others believed that the government,
having already agreed to build the northern Ontario section, would
be better advised to construct the whole pipe line than to submit to
demands from a United States-controlled corporation. By the spring
of 1956, however, the Liberal government had committed itself to the
support of Trans-Canada. By its refusal in 1953 to permit the export
of gas to the United States until the pipe line had been built to central Canada, the government had implicitly committed itself to assisting the construction of that pipe line by any means in its power.[30] The
position taken in 1953 could not be abandoned. On the other hand,
some export outlet for Alberta gas was indispensable. Continued
refusal to permit gas exports would seriously check the development
of the industry, retard the pace of exploration, and jeopardize the
political position of the Liberal party in the western provinces and
Ontario. The proposed loan to Trans-Canada was therefore submitted to the House of Commons and, by dint of rather high-handed
parliamentary tactics, carried to a successful vote.[31]

The situation at present (April, 1958) is that Trans-Canada has
completed its section from the Alberta-Saskatchewan border to Fort
William, Ontario, and the section between Toronto and Montreal.
Construction is in progress on the 675-mile northern Ontario section
to be owned by the Northern Ontario Pipe Line Crown Corporation,

---

largest American gas pipe line companies. Canadian Gulf alone held, in May, 1956,
about one third of all proven gas reserves in Alberta.

[30] The Minister of Trade and Commerce stated in the House of Commons: "The
requirement that Canadian markets so far as possible be first provided for is a requirement of national policy. If any disability were placed upon the development of
the gas industry by this national policy, it would be proper that this disability
be if possible counterbalanced . . . . Private enterprise alone faced serious difficulties
in financing a pipe line stretching across the sparsely-populated areas of northern
Ontario, a line from which relatively low returns on investment must be expected
during the period of building up the central Canadian market. Some kind and degree of public intervention appeared necessary and proper." *Hansard*, March 15,
1956.

[31] See: Grant Dexter, "Politics, Pipelines and Parliament," *Queen's Quarterly*,
LXIII (1956), 323-333. The Canadian government in this case found itself in
the politically embarrassing position of proposing large financial aid to an American-
controlled corporation because of the obduracy of an American regulatory agency.
The financial feasibility of the project depended upon securing the approval of the
F.P.C. for imports of Canadian gas at Emerson. Failure to secure such approval
made private financing impossible and compelled recourse to government aid.

and completion is expected by the end of 1958. Meanwhile negotiations continue for exports of gas from western Canada to the United States. The Tennessee Gas Transmission Company has contracted to purchase up to 200 million cubic feet per day from Trans-Canada for distribution in the United States. This contract is, however, conditional upon the approval of the Federal Power Commission, whose verdict has not yet been rendered, and upon favorable action by the Canadian government, which announced in the fall of 1957 that approval of further exports of gas to the United States would be delayed until such time as the Borden Royal Commission on Energy completed its report.[32]

The final direction of government policy toward natural gas is not yet clear. It is evident, however, that a monopoly position in the United States market as a whole is not to be hoped for, whatever may be the position in particular fuel-deficient areas. In these circumstances to stress Canadian needs and the construction of the necessary east-west transportation facilities makes good sense. The larger the internal market in Canada, the less likely is it that the industry will become dependent on United States outlets, and the stronger will be the bargaining position of Canadian interests when and if reliable export opportunities develop. It is worth noting, however, that the insistence on an all-Canadian route has entailed costs, both in time and in money. Reliance on government construction and subsidies reflects the inadequacy of private capital resources in Canada and the disinclination of United States capital to dance to the tune of Canadian nationalism.

IX

The four cases that have been considered—pulpwood, nickel, petroleum, and natural gas—have much in common. Each of them is a resource available in large quantities in Canada. All were initially developed by United States capital and entrepreneurship, with the aid of United States technology, to serve the United States market. In each of them Canadian government policy has been directed toward modifying in some degree the tendency for the later stages of processing, manufacture, and utilization to be located in the United States. Difficulties in the way of these policies have been many: the structure

[32] Royal Bank of Canada, Oil and Gas Department, *Bulletin No. 12* (Jan. 1, 1958).

of the United States tariff, favoring raw material imports and penalizing imports of manufactured and semimanufactured goods; the retaliatory power of United States producers, determined to retain control of the domestic market; the location of corporate control in the United States; the availability of alternative sources of supply; and the basic locational advantages of situating the intermediate and final stages of processing close to the market and to allied industries. Success or failure for Canadian policy in each case has depended upon the balance of bargaining power. Canadian bargaining power has been strong in cases where Canada was the only source of supply economically available to United States producers, giving Canada a semi-monopolistic position, and where other locational factors, such as low-cost energy resources, have reinforced the pull of raw materials. It has been weak in cases where other sources of supply were actually or potentially available, where the United States domestic market was dominated by United States producers, and where there existed no particular locational advantage favorable to Canada. In general Canadian policy has proved effective only where it has operated to reinforce other locational factors that could be expressed in terms of business costs, and to accelerate a transfer of production that would probably have taken place anyway, though more slowly. It has been ineffective in cases where no such basic locational pull existed.

In conclusion, some implications for policy may be suggested. Canada has so far devised no generally effective means of protecting export industries comparable to the tariff as a means of protecting home industries. Attempts to achieve a more diversified and industrialized economy by means of a protective tariff have been a qualified success, supported as they have been by the construction of a national transportation system along the east-west axis. Attempts to achieve the same objectives for export industries, oriented toward the United States market along the north-south axis, have, however, been fraught with difficulties. Many of these difficulties stem from the fact that Canadian economic development necessarily depends upon exploiting market and resource opportunities as they appear. The exploitation of these opportunities has involved extensive participation by American capital and entrepreneurship in Canadian industries and has tended to mold the structure of the Canadian economy into a pattern that complements the needs of the United States. There seems little likelihood that pressures of this kind will decrease significantly in the near future; they are too deeply embedded in the market and resource structures of the two economies to be banished by exhortation or by the fluctuating fortunes of political parties. Attempts to counteract these pressures involve real costs, not only in terms of international relations, but also in terms of retardation of the rate of economic development. Rapid economic growth in Canada has in the past depended largely upon the influx of capital and entrepreneurship from more advanced countries; there is little reason to suppose that this pattern can be quickly modified by government policy. The expansion of the internal market in Canada, the development of a manufacturing sector to serve that market, and the establishment of a strong and diversified resource base are likely to be more effective in modifying the pattern of Canadian dependence. These are, however, secular or long-run factors, not likely to produce dramatic changes within a few years.

2

Recent American Influence in Canada

With Particular Reference to Economic Factors and Canadian Reaction

JOHN J. DEUTSCH

I

Over the past century relations with United States became a major issue in Canadian politics at least once in every decade. The present decade is no exception. The nature and context of the particular political manifestations have varied with the circumstances and personalities of the time. These manifestations, however, have had their roots in basic political and economic developments which were seldom faced explicitly and rarely elucidated in political discussion. Again, the political expression of present Canadian anxieties is no exception. After the recent Canadian election a leading Canadian journalist commented:

American editorial writers do well to interpret the Diefenbaker landslide as an evidence of Canadian nationalism with some slight anti-American tinge . . . the degree to which the Diefenbaker victories both in June and March represented a reaction to the fear of domination by the United States deserves attention below the border where Canada has so long been taken for granted.[1]

It is the purpose of this paper to examine some of the fundamental forces and trends of American influences on Canada in the postwar period and then to relate these forces and trends to the fears and emotional reactions to which they gave rise. It is not my purpose to deal with the political tactics and personalities which have been such prominent features in popular discussion.

Twenty years ago Professor H. A. Innis described the nub of the basic problem in these succinct terms.

[1] J. Bird, *Canadian Commentator*, April, 1958.

Canada is facing to an increasing extent the effects of contrast between two systems. An old system linked her to Europe by a geographic background dominated by the St. Lawrence . . . . The new system links Canada to the United States and is evident in the increasing importance of exports from Canada to the United States . . . and in the rapid spread of inventions from the United States to Canada . . . . The conflict between the two systems has cumulative effects. Nationalism becomes more intense . . . . The politician is quick to seize upon the possibility of capitalizing hostility to either the United States or Great Britain, and Canadian nationalism flourishes under these conditions. . . .[2]

II

The Canadian economy began and developed as an outpost of Europe and Great Britain. The St. Lawrence and the Great Lakes served as the great artery of transportation for staple exports from the heart of the continent to overseas markets and as the highway for the movement of manufactured goods from Europe. During the latter half of the nineteenth century and the early part of the twentieth, this structure was elaborated into an east-west transcontinental system through the construction of transcontinental railways and the settlement of the West. The east-west flow of commerce was supported by a protective tariff which promoted the production of manufactured goods at the center and their sale in the outlying regions. The development of the east-west pattern and the export of primary staple products to overseas markets was strongly influenced also by the highly protectionist policies of the United States, which restricted the growth of north-south specialization on the North American continent.

During the latter part of the nineteenth century and up to the outbreak of World War I, close to 60 per cent, on the average, of Canadian exports went to Europe—very largely to Great Britain. These exports consisted mainly of food-stuffs and raw materials. The substantial amounts of foreign capital which were required for the settlement of the Canadian West came primarily from Great Britain. At the end of 1914 three-quarters of total foreign investment in Canada was British and less than one-quarter was American.[3]

The British- and European-oriented Canadian economy faced its first major problem of structural adjustment at the end of World

[2] H. A. Innis, *Essays in Canadian Economic History* (Toronto, 1956), pp. 235-238.

[3] See Appendix Table 9.

War I. The predominant position of Great Britain as the leading world creditor and trader was seriously weakened. The position of the United States as an economic and financial power was greatly enhanced. The increased influence of the United States upon Canada as a result of this change was heightened by a growing shortage of certain raw materials which Canada could supply: i.e., pulp, paper, and minerals. These new demands resulted in the rapid growth of large new primary industries in Canada based upon export to the United States. During the 1920's, as a result of these developments, the United States replaced Great Britain as the leading market for Canadian exports and as the leading source of foreign capital. Great Britain, nevertheless, continued to be a very important market, especially for agricultural products. The otherwise stronger economic attraction of the United States was limited, however, by a continued protectionist policy which resulted in successive increases in United States tariffs, culminating in the Hawley-Smoot tariff of 1930. The latter had a particularly severe effect upon Canada and consequently was an important factor in bringing about a substantial change in Canadian commercial policies. This change was embodied in the Ottawa Agreements of 1932, which established an effective preferential trading system within the Commonwealth. As far as Canada was concerned, this was accomplished mainly by sharp increases in duties against United States products. This action had the effect of reversing previous trends and resulted in some, though not substantial, diversion of Canadian exports and imports from the United States to Great Britain and other Commonwealth countries. One of the principal results of the Ottawa Agreements was the large increase in the protection afforded to Canadian manufacturing industries. At the same time preferential markets were opened up for Canadian manufacturers in Commonwealth countries. This brought about a new influx into Canada of United States branch plants to take advantage of the protected Canadian and Commonwealth markets.

However, the protectionist and Commonwealth orientation of the early 1930's did not continue in its full rigor for long. The passage of the Reciprocal Trade Agreements Act opened a new era in United States commercial policy, and Canada was quick to explore its possibilities. In 1935 Canada and the United States succeeded in negotiating their first comprehensive trade agreement since 1854-1866. Under this agreement Canada extended most-favored-nation treatment to the United States and obtained significant tariff reductions on exports of important primary products to the United States. This new departure was to have a substantial effect on the direction of Canadian trade.

III

This brief sketch of the background will serve to indicate the conflicting pulls which affected the Canadian economy on the eve of World War II. An analysis of this position is essential for an understanding of the Canadian international economic problems as they emerged at the end of the conflict. The principal features of the immediate prewar situation are shown in Appendix Tables 6, 8, 9, and 13.

These tables indicate that immediately prior to World War II Canadian exports were almost equally dependent upon United States and British markets. However, the United States occupied the predominant place as the source of Canadian imports and of foreign capital. This pattern indicated a considerable unbalance in the structure of international payments. The principal out-payments for imports and debt service went to the United States. The excess in payments to the United States was financed out of the net proceeds from exports to the United Kingdom and the rest of the world.

TABLE III

CANADIAN BALANCE OF PAYMENTS ON CURRENT ACCOUNT,
1937-1939 AVERAGES

Current Account Surplus (+) or Deficit (−) with:	$ millions
United States	−114
United Kingdom	+133
Other Commonwealth and Empire	+ 36
Other	+ 81
Total Current Account	+136

Source: See Appendix Table 13, which also gives data for other years.

Equilibrium in the Canadian balance of payments was achieved by a trilateral balancing of accounts. Broadly speaking, the current account deficit with the United States was met out of the surplus with Britain and other Commonwealth countries. This method of balancing was dependent upon a system of multilateral trade and convertible currencies. In particular, it was dependent upon the ready convertibility of the pound sterling into United States dollars.

At the end of World War II, as in the case of World War I, Canada once more encountered changed circumstances in its relations with its two dominant economic partners. This time, however, the changes were more serious and far-reaching. The economic position of Great Britain in the world was greatly weakened by the struggle. Great Britain had become a large debtor and had suffered a serious loss of markets. The United States, on the other hand, emerged as the world's strongest economic power. In contrast with Great Britain and other European countries, the productive capacity and the financial resources of the United States were substantially increased. Furthermore, these changes had been accompanied by a complete breakdown in the system of multilateral trade. Virtually all currencies, with the exception of the United States dollar, had become inconvertible. Great Britain and other Commonwealth countries, not including Canada, had established a common system of exchange and import controls under which payments to Canada and other dollar countries were closely rationed. Sterling, the leading currency of international trade, was no longer convertible. In the light of Canada's trading and balance of payments position as it existed before the war, the drastically altered circumstances posed critical problems in the formulation of Canadian postwar economic policy.

These problems had to be faced against the background of the severe depression and heavy unemployment which prevailed throughout the 1930's. The demands of the war had restored the Canadian economy to full operation and had brought about striking increases in industrial capacities. As the war drew to a close there loomed ever larger the question as to how adequate employment and future growth was to be achieved in the changed and disturbed conditions of the postwar world. History had shown that Canadian economic expansion had always been basically dependent upon the availability of expanding export markets, of modern techniques, and of adequate supplies of capital.

Policies of self-containment and self-sufficiency were policies of despair. Consequently the assurance and development of export markets on the widest possible basis was a primary objective of Canadian postwar policy. Immense difficulties stood in the way because of the ambivalent position of the Canadian economy between the United States and Great Britain and because of the need for a tri-angular balancing of the external accounts. Canada required a large and continuing market in Great Britain and Europe both as an outlet for foodstuffs and primary materials and as a source of exchange with which to finance a continuing deficit with the United States. How-ever, the ability of Great Britain and other European countries to pro-vide convertible exchange for purchases from Canada was strictly limited, while the demand for imports from the United States had increased, especially for investment goods required for an expanding Canadian economy. The concentration on imports from the United States was further enhanced by the difficulty of obtaining manufac-tured goods from the war-damaged economy of Great Britain. The structure of Canadian trade was more unbalanced than ever. The problem was how to resolve the conflicting tendencies while at the same time achieving an adequate impetus for economic growth.

The Canadian government sought the answer in a persistent at-tempt to re-establish a system of international trade and payments which would be favorable to Canada's position and would remove the predicament in which Canada found herself. The government stated its aims in the White Paper of April, 1945 as follows:

The Government is looking to an expansion of total world trade, within which other countries as well as Canada can increase their exports. The expansion of Canadian exports will be one phase of an expanded Canadian economy which will require for its use greatly increased imports . . . . The conditions under which postwar trade can reach higher levels than before the war are not, in any large degree, under the direct control of the Cana-dian Government. They must be achieved by collaboration with other governments, and particularly, in view of the direction of our trade, with the governments of the British Commonwealth and of the United States. . . . The Government has pressed and is continuing to press actively for a wide collaboration in the reciprocal reduction and removal of trade barriers, especially trade barriers of an arbitrary and discriminatory type . . . . Having regard to the widespread character of our trade, the Government attaches special importance also to the reconstitution of multilateral trade on a firm basis arrangements under which the proceeds of our exports may be spent wherever we desire to obtain our imports.[4]

To these ends the Canadian government played a leading part in

[4] *White Paper on Employment and Income* (Ottawa, 1945), p. 7.

the negotiation of agreements and in the development of international organizations designed to restore multilateral trade and the convertibility of currencies. Along with the United States, Canada took the initiative in the establishment of the Bretton Woods monetary institutions and in the negotiation of the General Agreement on Tariffs and Trade (GATT). The Canadian government held out high hopes for these achievements. In the case of the Monetary Fund it expected that the Fund "would outlaw the discriminatory currency practices which turned trade into economic warfare. When it was fully in operation, it would assure the convertibility of the proceeds of our sales abroad into whatever currencies we required for our current needs."[5]   In the case of GATT the Minister of Finance stated that "The ultimate objective of these negotiations is to make possible the restoration of multilateral trade on a large scale which is the best possible basis for Canadian prosperity and stability."[6]

In these initiatives the Government of Canada and the United States administration were active partners. Both shared the same concept of desirable international economic policy. There was close co-operation and understanding.[7] For Canada the common aims were especially congenial because the search for a broad basis of trade would relieve the conflicting pulls on the Canadian economy and would help to prevent excessive dependence upon either one of the dominant trading partners, particularly the United States.

On her part Canada proceeded to put her own precepts into practice. She adopted a liberal trade and economic policy. Wartime controls were dismantled as soon as possible and Canada refrained from the use of quantitative or discriminatory restrictions on her trade even though a substantial part of her export markets were in the sterling area and other overseas countries with inconvertible currencies. Instead Canada attempted, in respect of these countries, to apply an expansionist approach by encouraging imports from them and by extending substantial credits so that "Britain and the countries of western Europe, would be able to buy our food-stuffs, metals, other raw materials and some of our new manufactured products, in order to re-establish their economic life and emerge as great trading nations pro-

[5] *Ibid.*, p. 7.

[6] Hon. D. C. Abbott, *Budget Speech*, April 29, 1947 (Ottawa, 1947), p. 5.

[7] The position of the United States Congress, however, was less clear and consistent.

viding markets for our goods."[8] At home the Canadian government
sought to promote expansion through the encouragement of private
investment, both domestic and foreign. No impediments were put
in the way of the inflow of foreign capital—indeed it was welcomed
as a constructive and even necessary contribution to Canadian growth.

The hopes held out for the Canadian and United States international economic policies proved to be premature and overoptimistic.
The attempt to restore the convertibility of sterling in 1947 ended in
failure. This failure resulted in an intensification of trade restrictions
throughout the overseas world. In the autumn of that year Canada
herself encountered an exchange crisis. The proceeds of Canadian
exports to Britain and Europe, a large part of which was financed by
credits, were insufficient to pay for the sharply rising imports from the
United States. This situation resulted in the adoption of an emergency program of import controls which were to be removed as soon
as feasible.

These events made it clear that Canada's dependence upon a tri-
angular balancing of its external accounts would bring increasing difficulties in the postwar world. Consequently Canadian policy became
more directly concerned with the possibility of reducing this dependence through the achievement of closer bilateral balances, including
that with the United States. In particular, increased emphasis was
placed on the expansion of exports to that country. The alternative
of a substantial and permanent reduction of imports from the United
States by protectionist or arbitrary means was rejected. This alternative was held to be in conflict with desirable international economic
policy, seriously disruptive to large segments of the Canadian economy, and dangerous in respect of the desire for continued economic
expansion.

In these circumstances the pull of the United States on the Canadian economy was significantly increased while the influence of Great
Britain and Europe declined. The events of 1947 were followed by
sterling crises in 1949 and 1951. The outstanding success of the
Marshall Plan in promoting European recovery was not matched by
a corresponding progress in the restoration of multilateral trade and
convertibility of currencies. At all international discussions and con-
ferences Canada continued to be an enthusiastic and relentless advo-
cate of multilateralism and convertibility. However, the support of

[8] Hon. J. L. Ilsley, *Budget Speech*, June 27, 1946 (Ottawa, 1946), p. 5.

the United States became more unreliable and less and less effective owing to Congressional waverings and transgressions. Canadian efforts became tiresome to many and as yet have achieved only a limited success.

IV

The effects of postwar international economic developments upon the orientation of the Canadian economy toward the United States were intensified by a further important circumstance. This circumstance was reminiscent of what had occurred after World War I, but this time it was much more powerful. The war-expanded industrial capacity of the United States had made heavy drafts upon resources of raw materials with the result that domestic supplies in many cases became more and more inadequate. This situation was magnified by the demands of the Korean War and by the large rearmament program which has continued to the present day. The rising requirements of the United States could most easily be supplemented from the undeveloped resources of minerals, fuels, and forests of Canada. Authoritative studies, in particular the Paley Report, indicated that raw material requirements from foreign sources would increase in the future. These forecasts justified the heavy investments required to bring Canadian supplies into large-scale production.

Geographical proximity, the desire for security in the circumstances of the cold war, and the absence of impediments to foreign enterprise and foreign investment all gave Canada a decided advantage, in the eyes of the United States interests, over alternative foreign sources. In a number of important cases United States integrated enterprises wished to acquire additional assured supplies of raw materials and consequently provided the large amounts of capital required and retained direct control of the undertakings. When, shortly after the War, new discoveries indicated that the prairie provinces contained large pools of oil and gas, the huge United States international oil companies with their world-wide experience, know-how, and ready access to capital moved in on a large scale. This was facilitated by the fact that a number of these companies were already established in Canada and, also, by the fact that if Canadian production of oil and gas expanded sufficiently, outlets would have to be found in the United States in any case. The discovery in Canada

of immense resources of uranium coincided with the search by the
United States of adequate and assured supplies of this strategic material for the atomic energy program.

These circumstances and the increasing impact of United States
demands created a new and dynamic impetus to Canadian expansion.
The Canadian frontier moved northward and entire new areas were
brought within the sphere of economic development. During 1950-
1957 Canadian economic growth went forward at a rate faster than
at any time in history. The only other comparable period was the
wheat boom of 1900-1913. However, the bases of the two booms
were entirely different, and they had sharply contrasting effects. The
stimulus for the wheat boom came from Great Britain and Europe
and thus served to establish firmly the east-west structure of the Canadian economy. The stimulus for the boom of the 1950's came wholly
from the United States, with the result that the east-west structure
was fundamentally modified by an almost massive north-south integration. Toward the end of the period Canadian trade statistics revealed the emergence of almost entirely new exports to the United
States of iron ore, uranium, oil, and nonferrous metals which rivaled
and in some cases superseded in size the traditional staples which were
sold in overseas markets. The industries producing these staples
languished as their products came up against impenetrable protective
barriers and currency restrictions abroad. These conditions were not
confined to any one industry or region. For example, on the east
coast as the markets for salt cod in southern Europe were lost due to
currency restrictions, substantial new markets for frozen fillets were
found in the United States.

v

The American-generated boom of the 1950's made possible re-
newed economic growth on a wide scale. The population, supplemented by a substantial revival of immigration, increased at a rapid
rate. This expansion created immense requirements of new social
capital and of manufactured goods, both for consumption and investment purposes. Total new capital investment for housing, community facilities, utilities, resource development, and additional manufacturing capacity rose spectacularly. In 1957 total new capital investment increased to 28 per cent of GNP, one of the highest ratios in the

world. This level of investment was substantially in excess of the Canadian supply of savings. American investors responded quickly to the opportunities in a country where social conditions were stable, where the methods of business were similar and understood, where contacts and communications were easy, where there was a minimum of government control, where private enterprise was encouraged, and where foreign capital appeared to be welcome. The Canadian rate of growth and population increase were considerably greater than those of the United States and consequently many investors in the United States saw the possibility of a stake in the future and capital gain through investment in Canadian enterprises. This possibility was especially interesting in a period of inflation and therefore there was a considerable emphasis on investment in Canadian equities. Furthermore, American enterprisers had had a long experience in operating on the frontier and in wresting from it the riches of nature. The Canadian frontier became the North American frontier.

The inflow of capital from the United States began to rise steeply after 1952 and reached almost one billion dollars in 1956. The capital was invested mainly in resource-development projects, in equity securities, in manufacturing facilities, and to a lesser extent in bonds and government obligations. American industry was eager to expand its branch-plant operation in Canada in order to take advantage of a rapidly growing domestic demand and in order to make use of know-how and research in a market closely attuned to American styles, tastes, and promotional activity. The latter factors were especially important in a period when there was a rapid increase in the emphasis on research and methods of sales promotion. Under these various influences the degree of American ownership and control of Canadian industry increased steadily. In 1956 about one-third of total *net* capital formation in Canada was financed from abroad, close to three-fourths of which came from the United States. In that same year about one-quarter of total Canadian industrial investment was controlled by United States residents.

The inflow of capital was accompanied by a corresponding rise in imports from the United States and by a corresponding increase in the current-account deficit in the balance of payments with that country. The principal increase in imports consisted of capital goods and producers' materials required for the Canadian investment program. There was also some, but smaller, rise in imports of consumer goods.

In recent years nearly 90 per cent of the immense imports of capital goods into Canada were supplied by the United States because of the preponderance of American industrial methods in Canada, old established connections, and ready availability. Although close to three-quarters of all Canadian imports were obtained from the United States, the old problem concerning the triangular balancing of the external accounts had temporarily disappeared. It was submerged, for the time being, by a flood of capital.

VI

The nature and degree of the realignment of the Canadian economy in the postwar period are indicated by the statistics in Table IV. Some of the influences which have brought about these substantial shifts in the direction of the United States have been discussed above.

TABLE IV

CHANGES IN THE GEOGRAPHICAL DISTRIBUTION OF CANADIAN TRADE
AND FOREIGN DEBT FROM THE PREWAR PERIOD TO 1956
(In Percentages of Totals)

	EXPORTS		IMPORTS		FOREIGN DEBT	
	Average 1937-39	1956	Average 1937-39	1956	Average 1937-39	1956
United States	35	60	63	73	60	76
United Kingdom	38	17	17	9	36	17
Other Countries	27	23	20	18	4	7

Source: See Appendix Tables 6 and 9, which also give data for other years.

Among these was the failure, at least for the present, of the Canadian efforts to secure the restoration of multilateral trade and convertibility of currencies. Indeed, these efforts worked only in relation to the United States. Among the many tariff agreements which Canada negotiated at Geneva in 1947, only that with the United States achieved substantial results in reducing barriers to trade. The others were almost wholly nullified, as far as Canadian exports were concerned, by controls and currency restrictions. The preferences which continued to be accorded to Canada in other Commonwealth markets were also similarly nullified. The attempt to obtain a larger share of imports from Britain and Europe was frustrated by the claims for

postwar reconstruction and by the persistence of inflationary conditions overseas. The remarkable fact is that in spite of these disappointments, Canada received an impetus from abroad that brought
about unprecedented prosperity. However, this very prosperity, because of the exclusive source of this impetus in the United States, has
aroused feelings of nationalism and a desire for greater economic independence.

The high concentration of trade, borrowings, and ownership of
industry in the United States has created fears of being overwhelmed
by a giant neighbor whose population is eleven times as large and whose
national production is fifteen times as large as Canada's. Some Canadians have become seriously concerned over the question of whether,
in these circumstances, Canada can continue to be master of her own
economic destiny, or perhaps of her political destiny. These Canadians
point to the one-sided aspect of the relationship in that Canadian exports to the United States are equivalent to about 12 per cent of Canada's national income whereas United States exports to Canada are only
about 1 per cent of the national income of the United States. In these
circumstances it is felt that Canada has become unduly vulnerable to
United States policies, regardless of whether these policies are inspired by friendly, self-interested, or sinister motives. Those who
have this concern are not comforted when it is pointed out that a one-
sided economic relationship has been a Canadian fact of life throughout history and is likely to continue to be so for some considerable
time regardless of any possible changes in the early future.

When feelings of nationalism and fear are present together, there
are likely to arise antipathies and emotional confusions. These antipathies and confusions are present in some Canadian circles, and they
provide material for political exploitation. In this respect Professor
Innis' diagnosis has proved accurate. However, there are some rational and real causes for worry. The nature of these worries in
official quarters has been stated recently by the Canadian Minister
of Finance as follows:

Because of the vital place that external trade occupies in the Canadian economy, and the large proportion of this trade which is concentrated on the
United States, changes in the terms of access to the United States market,
even where they may be of minor importance in the United States scheme
of things, often have a critical significance to our country—a fact which
unhappily is not always appreciated in that country.

While access to the United States market has been improved in the last decade, and its tariffs have been significantly reduced, entry into that market remains difficult and uncertain for many classes of goods produced in Canada. In many cases, especially on fully manufactured goods, tariff rates are almost prohibitive. Quite apart from the tariff, their customs laws and administration often impose serious additional barriers. Perhaps most troublesome of all are the uncertainties arising from the many escape clauses in United States legislation and administrative practices.

Apart from direct restrictions imposed on Canadian agricultural products, we suffer severe harm from United States surplus activities. Massive United States disposals of wheat and other grains on give-away or subsidized terms have done serious damage to Canadian exports . . . . We find it difficult to understand why the United States should treat its best customer and friendly neighbor in this way.[9]

Canadians are anxious to achieve a dynamic and industrially diversified growth in the future. It will be recognized that in this Canadians have been strongly influenced also by the example of the United States. Canadians fear that their hopes in this respect may be frustrated by the existing United States commercial policies toward Canada and by the high degree of ownership of Canadian industry in the United States. The protective tariffs against manufactured goods and the virtual exclusion of any possibility for the development of a substantial two-way trade in such commodities has created fears that Canada will be cast permanently into the role of a mere supplier of raw materials to the United States, and perhaps a marginal one at that. Some aspects of the United States agricultural surplus disposal policy strike at an especially sensitive spot. The Canadian wheat industry has been the backbone of the east-west economy and the difficulties which this industry has encountered give rise to one of the most serious disappointments over the failure to restore an effective system of multilateral trade and payments. In these circumstances the intervention of the immense resources of the United States Treasury has been particularly frightening.

VII

Attitudes toward the recent American influence in Canada can easily fall into inconsistencies. On the one hand Canada has benefited

[9] Hon. Donald M. Fleming, *Budget Speech,* June 17, 1958 (mimeographed; Ottawa, 1958), pp. 14-15.

immensely from the dynamic influence and friendly disposition of the United States, but on the other hand these influences can also be frustrating to legitimate Canadian national ambitions, and can be damaging no matter how unconscious or unintended. It has become fashionable to cast blame for many of the frustrations and disappointments which have arisen in the disrupted postwar world upon the United States. Canada has had its share of disappointments, and some of these have related to the basic and historic structure of her economy and external orientation. It is necessary to maintain a balanced view. Such a balanced prescription was given in the Report of the Gordon Commission:

Such economic problems as may arise from time to time between the two countries would be eased, in our opinion, if more Americans could remember to think of Canada, not as a hinterland, but as a country. Canadians, for their part, while taking such action as may be necessary to provide the economic basis for the nation they are building in the northern half of the continent, would do well to recognize how much they have profited from having as neighbours a people so productive, so ingenious and so capable of magnanimity.[10]

[10] Royal Commission on Canada's Economic Prospects, *Final Report* (Ottawa, 1957), p. 55.

3

Canadian Economic Policy from 1945 to 1957—Origins and Influences

W. A. MACKINTOSH

I

Canadian economic policy has at all times been powerfully influenced by the experience of the United States in dealing with similar problems at much earlier stages. It has been colored by ideas from the United Kingdom and less frequently from other countries. To the degree that the policies of successive administrations have had coherence, they have been shaped to the stubborn facts of Canadian national life. In borrowing much of their land and railway policy from the United States and considerable elements of their social security measures from the United Kingdom, Canadians necessarily had to make modifications to fit differing and awkward Canadian conditions. Not infrequently the experience of other countries has been as useful in showing us what *not* to do as in providing us with a model.

It is necessary to an understanding of Canadian economic policy to know that, to an important degree, the federation and the Government of Canada were devised to provide an authority capable of planning and promoting national economic development and creditworthy enough to acquire the resources to finance it. The immediate project was to acquire a "West" for farm settlement and to link it by all-Canadian transport with the Pacific, the St. Lawrence, and the Atlantic.

Just as the federal government in the United States was powerfully strengthened by its control of the public domain, so the Canadian government found a source of strength and opportunity for initiative in its control of the territories of the west hitherto held by the Hudson's Bay Company. There was this difference, however. In the case of Canada, the acquisition and development of the public domain was a much more deliberately conceived reason for the establishment of a central government. Well into the 1920's land and railways were major instruments of national policy looking toward development. Indeed, it was not until 1930 that the remaining public lands were turned over to the provinces which had been created in 1905. In the next decade the emphasis changed, and it was found that the federal structure which had served reasonably well for coping with western development proved ineffective in attempting to deal with fluctuation and depression.

Since the separate colonies entered the Canadian federation in 1867, national economic policy has had two overriding concerns, growth and fluctuation. Until after World War I, the greater attention was concentrated on growth, partly because without development the economy could not become viable and the obstacles to growth were stubborn, and partly because fluctuations were deemed beyond control and matters for lament rather than policy.

The sharp crisis of 1920 and the depression which followed it drew attention to the importance of fluctuations but produced little in the way of considered policy. For six or seven years the problems of growth re-emerged, only to be overshadowed in the great depression of the 1930's. This depression, which combined in extreme form industrial and agricultural dislocations with catastrophic price declines, had an exaggerated impact on a country whose major exports were wheat, paper, and industrial materials. Unavoidably, Canadian governments, like those of most other countries, found themselves in a position in which economic fluctuation was the dominant fact of economic life.

After World War II, another period of growth set in, and for a decade concern with development was again paramount.

In any approach to the economic problems grouped under these two headings, consideration had always to be given to two limiting conditions imposed on Canadian economic policy: first, the federal structure of the country's government and, second, the extreme openness of the Canadian economy and its exposure to all the winds and currents of the economic world.

The problems of the federal structure are not our main concern here, but they cannot be entirely ignored since they thrust themselves into the major decisions of economic policy.

II

One of the earliest Commissions created to study the effects on economic policy of the federal structure and the openness of the economy was the National Employment Commission. It was established by statute in 1936 in recognition of the fact that "Unemployment has been for several years Canada's most urgent national problem." The Commission's main functions were to investigate and make recommendations on the conditions and organization of unemployment relief, proposals for public works programs and other employment projects, co-operation with commercial and industrial groups, and comprehensive measures on the long-range plans of national development. The more important recommendations of the Commission were directed to an attempt to disentangle financial assistance to the provinces from functional aid in dealing with the problem of unemployment.[1] This involved a recommendation that the federal government assume much larger financial and administrative responsibility for unemployment, both through the establishment of an insurance scheme and the setting up of a system of federal unemployment aid. This recommendation marked the beginning of a program under which the federal government assumed sole or major responsibility for those forms of assistance which could be provided through an insurance scheme or, as in the case of family allowances and old-age pensions, on a universal basis.

It was part of the Commission's recommendations that the haphazard role of conditional grants-in-aid should in future be minimized and replaced as far as possible by unconditional grants or those established on objective statutory terms. In this, the Commission was turning away from examples in the United States where federal aid was predominantly of a conditional type involving federal intervention in both state and municipal affairs. With modifications appropriate to circumstances, the pattern recommended by the Commission has been generally, though not exclusively, followed in Canada during the past twenty years. The preference for unconditional grants and single administrative responsibility was occasioned by a concern for the autonomy and budgetary responsibility of the provincial governments.

In reporting on the rôle of public expenditures in contributing to

[1] National Employment Commission, *Final Report* (Ottawa, 1938).

the stability of the economy, the Commission writing in 1937 was evidently strongly influenced by Keynes' *General Theory* as well as by discussions in the United States. But it was alert to the necessity of shaping its recommendations to fit the facts of the Canadian economy and, particularly, the influence on it of other economies. The point of view is indicated in the following paragraph:

It is of vital importance, also, that expansion of public expenditures should be so timed as to exercise the maximum beneficial effect. The early period of economic crisis and depression is one in which certain necessary readjustments must be made which will permit costs and prices, particularly those in the export trades, once more to come into profitable alignment. It is a period in which weak financial positions must be strengthened or liquidated, and misdirected investment abandoned. A proper programme for meeting the problem of unemployment, particularly in a country dependent on export trade as is Canada, necessitates, therefore, that the initial burden of unemployment should be borne by Unemployment Insurance and Unemployment Aid. Only after an initial period during which the position of the export industries readjusts itself, or in severe cases is readjusted by appropriate governmental and banking policy, i.e., when the period of desirable liquidation has passed and low interest rates have been established, should a programme of expansion of public expenditures be undertaken. It is sufficient in the initial period that governments should not violently contract expenditures, though this should not be understood to mean that governments should not continually strive for the most economical administration. Also, the case for expansion of public expenditures will be much stronger in Canada if expansion is already taking place in the large creditor countries, more particularly in the United States and Great Britain.[2]

It is of some interest now that this paragraph drew the criticism of Alvin Hansen, who, at the time, was acting as adviser to one of the provincial governments and who held the view that the expansion of public expenditures should be undertaken immediately at the onset of a depression (if one is clever enough to determine when this is) without waiting for readjustments to take place. It is questionable whether one can make as clear a distinction as Dennis Robertson once made between the primary and the secondary depression and, if one were considering a closed economy, Hansen's criticism would have been justified at least in part and perhaps wholly. The decisive condition which the Commission faced, however, was the extreme open-

[2] *Ibid.*, p. 35.

ness of the economy and the very limited scope which expansionary measures could have while export industries had not yet adjusted themselves, whether through cost reduction or exchange-rate change, to new conditions in the export market. The point has in fact more theoretical than practical interest since expenditure policies, even if undertaken as promptly as possible, are likely to be delayed in execution and effectiveness.

III

By the time the National Employment Commission was completing its report, the government had already appointed the Royal Commission on Dominion-Provincial Relations to examine and make recommendations on the manifold problems which had arisen in the operation of the federal system. Most of the matters occupying the Commission's attention and most of its recommendations concerned fiscal problems and are not relevant to our present purpose.

In general, however, the Royal Commission followed the thinking of the earlier Commission in recommending the transfer of governmental functions and administrative responsibility to the federal government where it was deemed necessary that the federal government should meet the financial cost. It rejected the alternative of a greatly extended system of conditional grants-in-aid. It also leaned toward the earlier Commission's view that wherever welfare expenditures could be met by insurance or by a general contributory system, they should be administered by the central government. Thus the Commission recommended that the federal government assume responsibility for the maintenance of the employable unemployed and of their dependents, and also that if a contributory old-age pension system should be established, it should be under the control of the federal government. In addition, it recommended not only that primary-industry and farm relief in the form of operating-cost advances should be borne by the federal government when it was on a large scale, but also that the Dominion should assume direct administrative and financial responsibility rather than render indirect assistance by way of advances to the provinces affected.

The report of the Royal Commission on Dominion-Provincial Relations which was submitted in 1940 was not in any important measure implemented because of disagreement among the provinces and because the circumstances of war made it possible for the federal government to impose the wartime financial agreements which, for the time being, met the most urgent problems. However, the enactment of the constitutional amendment transferring unemployment insurance to the powers of the Parliament of Canada and the passing of an act to set up a system of unemployment insurance in 1940 followed the recommendations of both of these Commissions.

In this area of economic policy within a federal system, the Canadian pattern has differed substantially from that in the United States. There has been an insistence on the minimizing of conditional grants and a corresponding preference for a transfer of functions whether by agreement or constitutional amendment. In some respects the problems of dealing with ten provinces with very unequal resources and financial strength are more difficult than the problems of dealing with forty-eight states where some measure of uniformity is inescapable. In the past at least, in some Canadian provinces administrative resources have been as meager as financial means. To impose on them the supervision necessary to insure proper administration of the functions financed by conditional grants would have violated the federal principle.

IV

As Canada approached the end of the war, problems of reconversion and reconstruction were intermingled with the concerns of long-term economic policy. In April, 1945, the Minister of Reconstruction, with the approval of the government, presented to Parliament a White Paper on *Employment and Income* which, together with the *Proposals of the Government of Canada* to the Dominion-Provincial Conference on Reconstruction in August, 1945, constituted an unusually comprehensive statement of economic and fiscal policy.[3]

The White Paper on *Employment and Income* was not conceived primarily as a series of promises and predictions as to future policy. It began with a statement that the government adopted as a primary object of policy the maintenance of a high and stable level of employment and income. This, however, was not looked upon as being more than a realistic recognition of what had become an obligation of every

---

[3] *Employment and Income with Special Reference to the Initial Period of Reconstruction* (Ottawa, 1945); Dominion-Provincial Conference on Reconstruction, *Proposals of the Government of Canada* (Ottawa, 1945).

government, not of choice but of necessity. The main object of the White Paper was to set out the problems which lay ahead and to create a public understanding of the extensive and highly important legislation which Parliament had passed during the war (mainly in the parliamentary session of 1944), and of the international commitments which the government had undertaken. In terms of the familiar divisions of gross national expenditure, it was pointed out that the efforts of the government to promote conditions conducive to multilateral trade and such legislation and commitments as membership in UNRRA, the Export Credits Insurance Act of 1944, the International Monetary Fund and the International Bank for Reconstruction and Development, the Agricultural and Fisheries Price Support Act of 1944, and the declared willingness of the government to extend credits to Commonwealth and allied governments to procure their import requirements from Canada, could be expected to maintain our exports through the period of the reconstruction.

In the field of private investment and particularly in respect of public encouragement to private investment, the White Paper drew attention to provisions in the budget of 1944 for minimizing the impact, on capital expenditures for reconversion and reconstruction, of wartime taxation. Provision had been made for writing losses backward or forward against profits, for charging to the profits of war years maintenance expenditures of a designated postwar year, and for depreciation rates ranging from half to double the regular rates at the taxpayer's option on new capital investment. These marked the beginning of a much more flexible fiscal approach to the taxation of business income which preceded the use of some similar devices in the United States.

The National Housing Act had been rewritten in expanded and more liberal form in 1944 and special provision had been made for veterans' housing. The government undertook to use its wartime controls while they were in existence to make possible a steady improvement in housing supply. For the less spectacular needs of farmers and other rural dwellers, the Farm Improvement Loans Act of 1944 provided for a general guarantee of bank credit to provide for expenditures on machinery and the extension of farm buildings and equipment.

A more novel piece of legislation was the Industrial Development Bank Act of 1944, which owed something to British thinking and also to the Reconstruction Finance Corporation, but in the main looked not to the clearing up of the financial debris of the depression but to the expansion of new small industries unable to qualify for conventional credit. Under the management of the Bank of Canada, this institution has performed an unspectacular but effective service not only in financing many new enterprises but in demonstrating to the chartered banks and other sources of investment the ways in which such enterprises could be financed.

For the maintenance of consumption expenditures, the White Paper pointed out that the Unemployment Insurance Act of 1940 and the much more revolutionary Family Allowances Act of 1944 would contribute substantially to the stabilization or expansion of consumers' expenditures. In a measure, the two Acts were supplementary in that the Family Allowances Act reduced, if it did not eliminate, the necessity of adjusting unemployment compensation, whether in insurance benefits or assistance according to the size of the wage earner's family, a necessity which had complicated and frustrated all previous arrangements for unemployment relief. Legislation, already enacted, providing a wide variety of benefits for ex-service men would also help to maintain consumption expenditures.

It was forecast that if agreements could be reached with the provinces, the government was prepared to contemplate plans for contributory old-age pensions and for health insurance.

In respect of public investment, it was emphasized that private investment would still be by far the major factor in the investment field and further that federal investment expenditures had not in peacetime been as important as provincial and municipal expenditures combined. In general, the emphasis of the Paper was on sensible management of public investment projects so that they might make the maximum contribution to stability of employment and income, with the federal government undertaking advance planning of its own projects and offering encouragement and inducement to provinces and municipalities to do the same. Special emphasis was laid on the need for increasing expenditures on the development and conservation of national resources and on co-operation with the provinces in this field.

As to fiscal policy, the government pointed out that, during the war, by rigorous taxation, by reduction in the rate of interest, and by the full use of resources it had been able to keep the cost of debt charges down to about the same relative weight as they had in 1939. It considered, therefore, that it approached the postwar period with considerable freedom and would be quite prepared under threat of unemployment "to incur the deficits and increases in the national debt resulting from its employment and income policy, whether that policy in the circumstances is best applied through increased expenditures or reduced taxation. In periods of buoyant employment and income, budget plans will call for surpluses. The government's policy will be to keep the national debt within manageable proportions and to maintain a proper balance in its budget over a period longer than a single year."

This statement did not extend to the proposition that deficit financing was an exclusive or, even in all circumstances, a necessary element in combating unemployment. It attempted merely to state in unalarming terms the prudent view that if deficits had to be incurred, it was much more helpful to incur them in years of deficient employment when they would be a help rather than in the buoyant years when they would feed inflation.

There was nothing either radical or novel in the White Paper of 1945. Its intention was to contribute to a widespread understanding of measures which had already been put in motion and to do so by putting them in a coherent framework of thinking which would inspire the confidence necessary to carry through the major tasks of reconstruction.

Viewed from the point of view of the present, one can see that it was aimed to a large extent at the fear in the popular mind, which also pervaded business circles very widely as the end of the war approached, of a return to the conditions of 1939. It was conceived to be a reasoned exposition of the changes in legislation and circumstances which made such a return unnecessary and improbable. The ideas which gave coherence to the White Paper were common property in the United States, the United Kingdom, Canada, and other parts of the world. Their acceptance in Canada was aided by the fact that deficit-financing had not become an issue of political dissension as in the United States and there had been no extreme version of full-employment policy put forward as by Sir William Beveridge in the United Kingdom.[4]

In one respect, at least, the White Paper was deficient. It made

[4] W. H. Beveridge, *Full Employment in a Free Society* (London, 1944).

clear that there were very substantial dangers of postwar inflation and that anti-inflationary measures would have to be continued for some time. There is no doubt, however, that, though the warning of the dangers of inflation was clear, the reality of postwar inflation turned out to be much greater than was forecast.

V

The *Proposals of the Government of Canada* to the Dominion-Provincial Conference on Reconstruction in August, 1945 (which came to be known as the Green Book), constituted essentially Part II of the White Paper on Employment and Income. The proposals concerned not only Dominion-provincial financial arrangements to replace the wartime taxation agreements but also all those measures for promoting a satisfactory level of employment and income which involved co-operation between the Dominion and the provinces.

More specifically, the Government of Canada proposed "to institute a system of managing its capital expenditures so that they may contribute to the maximum to the improvement of stabilization of employment and income and to work out arrangements by which the provinces, and to some extent the municipalities, might co-operate effectively and advantageously in such a programme."

The federal government attached special importance to expenditures which would conserve and develop the nation's natural resources, and particularly such expenditures in nonurban areas as would prove a substitute for declining incomes of primary industries. It noted that the bulk of the prospective expenditures in or near urban areas fell within the powers of the provinces and municipalities. It was proposed, therefore, that the federal government itself should extend its own work in surveying, planning, and research to make possible the acceleration or retardation of resource development programs and undertake the development and conservation of certain interprovincial river-valley or watershed resources as well as developing national transportation facilities. It offered to negotiate agreements for assisting the provinces to raise their standards in the work of conservation and development in agriculture and forestry, in providing access roads for mining and forestry, and in transport facilities of national importance. It offered also to participate in national programs for technical education and for the provision of the necessary hospital facilities for the ultimate adoption of national health insurance.

In this it was clear that the federal government deemed that the provinces independently did not have adequate resources to cope with the problems of employment on a concerted basis. In order that the provinces might be induced to come into a program in which the federal government controlled the timing, grants for the making of advanced plans were offered and it was proposed that timing grants amounting to 20 per cent of the cost of the projects should be given on planned and registered provincial projects which were undertaken at times approved by the federal government.

In the field of welfare and income maintenance, it was proposed that the federal government should establish old-age pensions universally for those 70 or over on the basis of contributions or a special tax. Pensions for those between 65 and 69 were to be provided on a means-test basis with the province and the federal government sharing the cost equally. Unemployment insurance was to be extended rapidly to include as many as possible of the labor force and an agreement was to be worked out with the provinces based on some formula which would result in the Dominion paying substantially the full cost of assistance payments to employable unemployed.

In the same field, the national government offered major participation (on the estimated costs, more than 60 per cent) in the progressive development of comprehensive health insurance and a series of health grants to provide a solid and more uniform base of health services.

In the event, the old-age pension proposals were implemented but, thirteen years later, health insurance is just now coming into effect in the much restricted form of hospital insurance. In part, costs much more formidable than the estimates of 1945 have deterred governments. In part, the task of building up health services has proved more extensive than anticipated.

The proposals of the White Paper and the Green Book were designed to place the Government of Canada in a position of leadership and effective control in policy related to economic development and fluctuation. This was the position designed for it at Confederation and which it held in the beginning in respect of economic development. They were also designed to make possible the extension in a federal state of a comprehensive system of social security measures with sound financial and administrative arrangements. Experience of other countries offered helpful suggestions, but the problems, though not exclusively Canadian, emerged from a Canadian background and had to be met with Canadian solutions. The proposals, on the whole, were shaped by Canadian ideas of federalism not identical with those of the United States. In adopting flat minimum standards for social security measures, other than unemployment insurance, and universal application, they followed British rather than American experience.

VI

External trade and finance were given a large place in the White Paper but furnished no more than a background to the proposals of the Green Book since these matters were entirely the responsibility of the national government and did not require provincial agreement.

From 1942 on, the Government of Canada had pressed strongly for postwar international arrangements which would increase the freedom of movement of trade and capital. Realizing the extent to which international trade contributed to our national income and the import of capital had assisted national development, the government pressed strongly for the elimination of all extraordinary and bilateral trade restrictions and control of capital movements such as had made the decade of the thirties so destructive of international economic relations. Increased freedom and multilateral trade were the major points of the Canadian case. The major obstacles to progress along these paths turned out to be the reliance and, at times, necessary reliance, of the United Kingdom on exchange control for the maintenance of the value of the pound, and, second, the rigid pattern and political entanglements of the United States trade agreements program. The whole pattern of what emerged as the General Agreement on Tariffs and Trade was determined by the relations between the President and the Congress and resulted in a form which found its justification in expediency rather than logic. There was difficulty also in what seemed to Canadians the almost theological attitude taken by the United States administration toward tariff discrimination and in favor of dealing unformly with both high-tariff and low-tariff countries.

In the event Canadians accepted the compromises and, over the intervening years, they have been strong, if sometimes complaining, supporters of GATT. The many escape clauses have meant that the commitments made by the United States are always less than firm and in no case have the tariff reductions been such as to enable Canadian secondary manufacturers to find any substantial or reliable market in the United States. Promised reform of the United States customs administration has been repeatedly deferred.

VII

The Canadian policy which was set out in the White Paper of 1945 and the Dominion proposals of the same year was a policy for the future which in a substantial measure had already been put in train except for those parts of it which involved provincial agreement. It is not the purpose of this paper to trace the difficult course of Dominion-provincial negotiations and agreements over the intervening years. It is sufficient to say that with a good many compromises and exceptions, they have followed out the main line of the proposals. Since 1945 an expanded provision for old-age pensions and currently an instalment of health insurance, limited to hospital and diagnostic services, have been added to unemployment insurance and family allowances. The proposals on public investment have been implemented only to a very limited extent in terms of certain federal and joint projects. In part, buoyant employment decreased the interest in the proposals. In part, their implementation required a radical overhaul of the federal Department of Public Works, which has now been substantially accomplished. That government has remained the dominant partner in the taxation of incomes, both personal and corporate, and the provincial governments have been given shares which have remained fixed or governed by a formula for five-year intervals. On the whole, the main lines of the policy have been followed as far as any forecast is, in a practical world, likely to be followed. Indeed, the remarkable thing is that the program laid down in 1945 has carried on as long as it has.

This is the more remarkable because the circumstances of the thirteen years since the end of the war have been quite different from any that were anticipated. Try as they may to look forward, most policy makers unavoidably look backward. Much of what was devised was shaped to avoid the mistakes and penalties of the 1930's.

Though the dangers of inflation in contrast to those of unemployment were emphasized at some length, they were, in terms of the realities of the postwar period, not emphasized nearly enough. No one foresaw the unusually rapid increase in population, the extensive Canadian developments in the fields of metals, oil, chemicals, and forest industries which have, in fact, taken place. No one forecast so large and persistent a capital investment and no one contemplated import deficits of the magnitudes which actually resulted. And yet, except for the universal error of attempting to do too much in too short a time, the policy turned out to be not ill adapted to the facts.

It was clear, however, by 1956 that there was some demand for a rethinking of policy. Creeping inflation was a persistent evil. The provincial agreements had never been extended to all provinces. The federal government came to the position where it apologized for its surpluses. Many questioned whether trade policy could proceed further along the current lines and there were misgivings as to the extent of the United States control of Canadian industry.

VIII

The Royal Commission on Canada's Economic Prospects, which was appointed in 1955, had strikingly different terms of reference from those of any previous Canadian commission. It was not asked for specific recommendations on policy but rather to examine the reasonable expectations of the economy over the next twenty-five years in respect to raw materials and energy, growth and distribution of population, growth and change of external and domestic markets, trends in productivity and standards of living, and requirements of industrial and social capital. It was also asked to report on the problems which such development appeared likely to occasion. The Commission, therefore, was free to make such recommendations as it saw fit but its obligations did not extend beyond the examination of the prospects and the identification of some of the problems.

In general, the Commission's report did not take serious issue with policies within the framework of the White Paper and the Green Book, though it did suggest changes in detail, pointed out some new problems which had arisen, and expressed the opinion that particular policies in some instances had about run their course. Of some other government policies it was more critical and made more radical recommendations.

It accepted the view of the White Paper of 1945 that the federal government must unavoidably accept the maintenance of a high level of employment and income as a major object of government policy and must cope with the recurring problems of inflation which might be inseparable from that obligation.

It commended the various instruments and practices which had been built up over the past fifteen years, such as the establishment of unemployment insurance, other social security payments, the use of tax concessions and flexible depreciation allowances to encourage investment and generally the practice of cyclical budgeting, including attempts to use tax concessions or increased expenditures to counteract unemployment.

It did point out, however, that despite the progress which had been made, the problems of coping with unemployment and inflation had been by no means solved, that the instruments in use were blunt and the art of using them still new. It strongly emphasized that both monetary and fiscal measures had to be used in concerted fashion and the problems of combining them were difficult and complex. It pointed out the need for more popular and business understanding of these problems and the relevant policies.

The Commission asserted the need in this field for strong federal authority because it seemed obvious that ten provincial governments could not be expected to act with concerted measures. On one point it was willing to borrow from the experience of the United States and suggested the advisability of a body of experts somewhat like the Council of Economic Advisers to the President, who could provide for needed public and legislative discussion periodic analyses of short-run economic prospects in a fashion which would not be appropriate or practical for permanent civil servants or members of a government.

In one sector of the field we have been considering, the Commission felt that postwar policy had about run its course. With much qualification and balancing, it stated its view that while progress might be made in particular areas, the prospects for further general liberalization of world trade were not promising. While acknowledging the hopes of the Common Market in Europe, it felt that further progress in relation to the United States was likely to be slow and meager. It advised, therefore, that, while the Canadian tariff needed to be revised and modernized, it should on the average be maintained at the present level. It contended that to press further with reciprocal tariff reductions would jeopardize secondary manufacturing in Canada, already faced with the double obstacles to expansion: *viz*, mass production for a much larger market in the United States and plentiful labor and low wages in Europe and Asia.

Though not specifically mentioned in the Commission's terms of reference, there was in the background at the time of its appointment concern about the overpowering influence of the United States in the conditions of Canadian life and the conduct of Canadian affairs.

This concern has arisen not from any anti-Americanism which is more than the normal sensitivity of a small neighbor. It arises from a great variety of sources of which three groups are perhaps the most significant. First, there are a number of specific points at which United States subsidiaries or branch enterprises are alleged to operate with special differential advantages. An illustration is in the oil industry, where the unusual generosity with which the United States tax authorities treat the petroleum industry when combined with Canadian reciprocal tax arrangements allegedly places United States exploration companies operating in Canada in a much more advantageous position than their Canadian competitors. The situation presents a familiar Canadian dilemma. Should it be rectified by adopting for the Canadian petroleum industry the American policy, which many Canadians think to be overgenerous, or should we in form discriminate against United States companies in order to achieve in fact a more equal balance?

In the second place, there is some concern over the dominant or even exclusive position of American corporations in certain Canadian industries. Any evidence that American policies are being extended to Canadian operations in contrast with differing Canadian practices gives rise to resentment. The resentment which Sir John Macdonald expressed when Canadian contentions about the Atlantic fisheries were sacrificed in the Treaty of Washington to bolster up the weak British case against the "Alabama claims" is an almost exact counterpart of the resentment which Canadians feel when their automobile industry becomes a testing ground for the vastly more important United States negotiation between the motor companies and the United Automobile Workers.

In the third place, there has been a frequent and repeated feeling of frustration at the limitation which American policy and the ways of the United States Congress impose on Canadian action. The whole postwar tariff program, in which Canadians had taken a leading and on the whole helpful part, ultimately ran in a pattern determined by the relations between the President and Congress and has recently reached a condition almost of stalemate. The development of the St. Lawrence, the development of hydroelectric energy in British Columbia, the exploitation of the resources of the Yukon, the distribution of western oil and gas, all these and many other projects get involved in American patterns and in American sectional politics.

On many of the specific items in these categories, the Royal Commission in its preliminary report in January, 1957, made specific suggestions for solving or easing the problems, but it is clear from the Commission's report that there is no single or simple solution. To a greater extent now than before, we cannot live without the American economy and we are never likely to be able to live in uninterrupted comfort or complacency with it.

IX

Canadian economic policy is always unavoidably influenced by United States thought and policy. In the first place, these are as basic, though not as predictable, as the conditions imposed by geology or climate. Whether the matter under consideration be trade, capital, or monetary policy, the United States' influence cannot be ignored.

In the second place, in many areas United States experience has preceded Canadian. From the building of railways to exploration for petroleum or gas, we have taken advantage of the experiments and achievements of the United States. In some cases we have been able to select the better among the practices and policies available for borrowing. In others we have selected almost outworn devices and schemes of organization.

Thirdly, our economy is closely, increasingly closely, geared to that of the United States. We need United States markets. We need United States capital. We need United States industrial "know-how." Clearly our economic policy will be shaped by our needs.

Yet there are other conditions and influences. The facts of Canadian economic life differ significantly from those of the United States. Our scattered population, lack of depth from south to north, the position of the Atlantic provinces thrust far to the north east, the great area of the Canadian Shield, the North with its perma-frost—these give us heavy national overheads much of which must be borne by the national government. It is true that we are at a much earlier stage of development than the United States but that should not be taken to mean that we will repeat all the steps by which the United States progressed.

Our conditions and our experience have given us somewhat different attitudes. Scarcity of capital and formidable obstacles to development and unity have made us look on government enterprise as a practical device for meeting special problems rather than the result of an ideological deviation.

Our history shows no sharp break with the United Kingdom and Europe and, despite the important enlargement of the Asian market, we are still dependent on them for cereal markets.

Being at an earlier stage of development, with the possibilities of secondary manufacturing industry restricted by the United States tariff, we have and will continue to have a greater stake in world trade than the United States. One of the significant features of the substantial Canadian development since the war is that it has not greatly modified our peculiar dependence on massive exports.

The Government of Canada was created to give initiative in economic development; now it must also give a similar initiative in coping with economic fluctuations and indeed with all phases of activity where our national welfare and identity are at stake. There will be variations and retreats and convenient compromises; but in the long run there will be no persistent division between parties on this score. Anti-American, antiforeign, or narrowly nationalistic policies are likely to be short-lived, but broadly national policies founded on the need for the protection and development of what is distinctively Canadian will be persistent. Any illusions that so open an economy can be subject to close and precise control will also be short-lived. Co-operation with the other nations on broad-based policies contributing to economic stability will be readily given and eagerly sought.

Economic policy since the war, however, has to a degree been based on the conviction that, though subject to the vagaries of wind and tide, there is still scope for navigation.

4

The Impact of United States Farm Policy on Canadian Agriculture

Clarence L. Barber

In RECENT YEARS Canadian newspapers have carried frequent stories about the effects of United States surplus disposal policies on Canadian wheat exports and have issued dire warnings that these adverse effects could be expected to continue well into the future. In these complaints and predictions they have been joined by politicians and by economists in business and university circles.[1] Nor have these complaints gone entirely unnoticed in the United States. Only last May Senator Morse accused Canada of "gross injustice" for suggesting that United States wheat sales to underdeveloped countries were depriving Canada of markets.[2] He defended the surplus disposal program on the grounds that it was creating a taste for wheat in rice-eating communities and hence developing a long-term market for wheat. Thus, whatever the truth of the matter, there can be little doubt that the actual or suspected effects of this particular aspect of United States farm policy has been a source of contention if not embitterment in Canadian–United States relations. Other features of that policy, such as the quota restrictions that have been imposed at times on Canadian oats, rye, and other products, have had similar though less severe effects. It becomes important, therefore, to establish as clearly as possible the facts in this situation.

I

The history of United States farm policy falls into two main periods.[3] Up until about 1929 farm policy was characterized by govern-

---

[1] See, for example, the two following articles: Lucy I. Morgan, "Exporting the U. S. Farm Surplus," *The Canadian Banker*, LXIV (1957), 87-99, and G. E. Britnell, "Implications of United States Policy for the Canadian Wheat Economy," *Canadian Journal of Economics and Political Science*, XXII (1956), 1-16.

[2] C. Knowlton Nash, "Don't Infuriate Canadians by 49th State Implications," *The Financial Post*, May 24, 1958, pp. 18-19.

[3] See W. W. Wilcox, "The American Farmer in a Changing World," *United*

ment support for agriculture through education, experimentation, and research and through the improvement of credit facilities. But with very few exceptions there was no attempt to intervene directly in the market. Prices and outputs were allowed to reflect market forces. A major change in this respect came with the creation of the ill-fated Farm Board in 1929. Although its purchase and loan operations proved insufficient to stabilize market prices, it was soon to be followed by more extensive market intervention. Production controls, acreage quotas, and support of prices through the nonrecourse loans of the Commodity Credit Corporation were all added to the government's farm policy program in the thirties. The most basic feature of this policy has been the parity price system under which the farmer is guaranteed a return equal to some fixed percentage of parity by an arrangement whereby the government takes over and holds off the market any supplies that cannot be sold at the support price. In the main this program has been confined to a number of basic storable commodities such as wheat, corn, rice, tobacco, cotton, and peanuts. In order to avoid the excessive accumulation of stocks which such a program tends to induce, the price-support plan has been supplemented by acreage controls and, more recently, by a soil bank program designed to take acreage out of production. Despite these attempts to curb production, stocks have continued to mount and the United States has recently been attempting to dispose of these surpluses by sales for soft currency, by barter arrangements, or by outright gifts to countries in need. The stated intention of the latter program is to increase the total volume of farm products moving through international trade channels by developing new market areas. Regular commercial sales by the United States and her competitors in international markets are supposed not to be affected.

II

These farm policies may affect other countries such as Canada in a number of different ways. Since it is difficult to keep commercial and noncommercial markets completely separate, surplus disposal programs run the risk of undermining regular commercial markets. This is true not only of the markets of foreign competitors of the United

States Agriculture: Perspectives and Prospects, The American Assembly (New York, 1955), pp. 11-26.

States such as Canada but also of the commercial markets of the United States herself. Further, when prices in the United States are supported at levels that exceed those in the world market, the government must resort to subsidies in order to export even to normal commercial markets. But once exports become dependent on government subsidization the entire export program comes under government control. By varying the size of the subsidy the United States government can compete more or less severely in the commercial markets of the world. It can also co-operate with a few other major suppliers in maintaining world market prices well above the levels that would prevail if markets were completely free, a fact that has been of some importance for Canadian wheat marketing. Again, price support programs must frequently be supported by import quotas to prevent the increased flow of imports that will be attracted by the higher prices. Even if imports are limited only to the volume that would occur in the absence of any market intervention, the quotas are likely to be misunderstood and may become a source of international friction. In practice, the quotas imposed are more severe than this. The importer may be required to share with the domestic producer on some pro rata basis the reduction in sales that results from the higher domestic prices. This is the practice stipulated by Article XI of the General Agreement on Tariffs and Trade. However, there have been frequent complaints from Canada and other countries that the import quotas on farm products imposed by the United States have not conformed to this provision. The United States has tacitly admitted the truth of this convention for in the GATT meetings of 1954-1955 she asked for and received a special waiver of this provision. Her import restrictions which are related to agricultural price support programs need no longer conform to the requirements of Section XI of GATT.

III

In attempting to judge the effects of United States farm policies on Canadian agriculture no consideration will be given to the situation that would exist in the complete absence of government intervention, including the pre-1929 type of U. S. farm policy, since the latter type of policy is all but universally accepted. Discussion here will be confined to the effects of policies which involve more direct interference with market prices and outputs.

One alternative to the present situation would be a continuance of the existing price-support policy, but without the surplus disposal operations carried out under the authority of Public Law 480. Such a policy probably implies acreage restrictions severe enough to prevent any surpluses from arising and perhaps also a reduction in the level of support prices. Another alternative would be to eliminate not only the surplus disposal policy but all direct government intervention in the market. Still another alternative would be the substitution of deficiency payments for price supports. Under this plan prices would be allowed to find their own level on the market but farmers would receive a deficiency payment equal to the difference between the guaranteed support price and the market price. Such a program might or might not be accompanied by production or acreage controls. The impact of United States farm policy on Canadian agriculture will be judged in terms of the situation that would exist if each of the above alternative policies were pursued. In each instance two important questions arise. How have Canada's agricultural exports to the United States market been affected? What has been the effect on Canadian exports to other areas? To these a third could perhaps be added: What have been the effects of these policies in Canada's own market? However, since Canada can easily protect her own market by the use of dumping duties this question will not be explored further.

IV

Analysis of this problem is complicated by the extent to which United States and Canadian exports of farm products during recent years have been financed, either directly or indirectly, by various forms of United States economic aid. Under the offshore purchase arrangements which were permitted in the early years of the Marshall Plan, some Canadian exports of wheat and other farm products were financed directly by United States economic aid. In later years this was no longer permitted but the general easing of the dollar problem which United States economic and military aid permitted undoubtedly eased the dollar situation of many countries and may have made it possible for them to buy more Canadian farm products than might otherwise have been the case. It is impossible, however, to get any precise measure of the importance of this factor to Canadian exports. But in the much easier dollar situation that exists today it seems safe to conclude that United States aid now has little if any significance. Moreover, in more recent years, United States aid has often been tied directly to the sale of surplus farm products. This would more than offset any favorable effects of this aid on the general dollar situation insofar as the export of most Canadian farm products is concerned.

Though many of the present features of United States farm policies have been in effect since the early thirties, it is only recently that they have had any significant effect on Canadian agriculture. Prior to 1938 price supports were confined to corn, cotton, tobacco, and naval stores. Of these products only tobacco is exported by Canada. Even when price supports were applied to wheat in 1938 they were initially at only 52 per cent of parity.[4] Thus in this period United States farm policy was primarily domestic in its effects. During the war and postwar periods the shortage of most foodstuffs kept prices of farm products at or above support levels most of the time so that problems of export subsidization, import quotas, and surpluses either did not arise or were of only brief duration. But within the past few years import quotas, fees, or informal restraints have been imposed on numerous products; and beginning in 1954 the United States embarked on a vigorous surplus disposal policy.

In the main the Canadian farm products which have been affected have been wheat and wheat flour, coarse grains, dairy products, flaxseed, potatoes, and honey. Of these by far the most important has been wheat. Before turning to an examination of these effects, however, it will be useful to examine in some detail the background of the Canadian wheat and coarse-grain situation. This discussion will be confined to production and marketing in western Canada, the area where the bulk of Canada's export supplies of these products originates.[5]

Canada first became an important wheat producer with the rapid settlement of the prairies during the first two decades of this century. Her total wheat acreage increased from about 5 million acres in 1905

[4] See *Price Programs*, Agriculture Information Bulletin No. 135, U. S. Department of Agriculture (Washington, 1957).

[5] This section draws heavily on D. S. MacGibbon, *The Canadian Grain Trade, 1931-1951* (Toronto, 1952).

returns for all wheat delivered to the Canadian Wheat Board during the period were to be averaged out at a uniform level. Prices for the two final years of the agreement were eventually set at $2.00 a bushel; this price also was below the free market export price during the two years it was in effect.

From the Canadian wheat producer's standpoint the agreement proved a bad one. At the time it was signed Canadian government officials were apparently anticipating a rapid recovery in European production and an early return of the surpluses and low prices that had characterized the prewar period. But as events turned out, Canadian farmers were forced to sell some two-thirds of all their exports during this period at prices that were at times as much as $1.50 per bushel below the free export price. Over the four-year agreement the loss to the farmers has been variously estimated at from $330 million to $600 million. The federal government eventually made a payment of $65 million out of general revenues as a compensation for the sacrifice that had been incurred.

Though on a lesser scale, the western Canadian farmer suffered a similar experience under the first International Wheat Agreement. During the first three years of the agreement, world prices averaged from 13 to 45 cents a bushel above the maximum prices under the agreement and the Canadian wheat producer absorbed this loss. In contrast, in the United States this difference between world market and Wheat Agreement prices was absorbed by a subsidy from the federal treasury, the farmers receiving either the full free market price or the support price if the latter was higher.

Because the western Canadian farmer never received the full benefit of the high prices that prevailed on world markets during the early postwar years, one might have supposed that he would not have had the same incentive to expand his wheat acreage as was true of the United States wheat farmer. Yet the statistics give only moderate support to this thesis. The largest acreage of wheat seeded in Canada since the war, 27.4 million acres in 1949, was only about 9 per cent higher than the 1935-1939 acreage of 25.6 million acres. Despite the apparently greater incentive for expansion faced by the American farmer, the wheat acreage seeded in the United States in the peak postwar year, some 83.9 million acres in 1949, was up only some 15 per cent over the 1935-1939 average—not greatly in excess of the increase that occurred in Canada.

To sum up, Canadian wheat farmers have received less favorable treatment pricewise than their American counterparts. Not only have they failed to receive the generous subsidies enjoyed by the latter, but at times they have failed to enjoy even the full free market price for their product. While the Canadian Wheat Board offers a method whereby the government could guarantee the farmer a price above free market levels and it was so used in the late thirties, since that time the government has, for the most part, avoided setting initial delivery payments high enough to provide any subsidization to the farmer. Only recently has there been some modification of this approach. Beginning in August, 1955, the government agreed to absorb the carrying charges on surplus wheat stocks, surplus stocks being defined as any carryover in excess of 178 million bushels in the hands of the Canadian Wheat Board at the end of the crop year. A year later provision was also made for modest advance payments on grain in storage on the farm. The marked difference between wheat prices received by wheat producers in Canada and the United States is evident from the data given in Appendix Table 15.

v

Two other features of the current situation in Canada deserve attention. First, unlike wheat farmers in the United States, Canadian wheat producers are not subject to acreage quotas that restrict the amount they can seed. Referring to this fact, Senator Humphrey has suggested that Canadians are in no position to criticize the United States surplus disposal program since they have done nothing to restrict their own acreage.[6] In fact, however, Canadian producers are and have been for some time sharply restricted through delivery quotas in the amount they can deliver to the Canadian Wheat Board. As of March 31, 1958, there were still 451 million bushels of wheat on Canadian farms which producers were unable to sell because existing commercial storage space was completely filled. Since the Canadian government has not taken steps to build additional storage space in the face of a mounting surplus, the surplus grain has simply backed up on the farm. The pipelines are so full that a decline in Canadian

[6] According to one press report, Senator Humphrey stated that "Canadian farmers have no production controls whereas U. S. farmers do and therefore Canada has been producing all the wheat she wants, which has not helped the surplus problem." Nash, *op. cit.*, p. 19.

exports is reflected almost immediately in a corresponding reduction in the farmer's ability to deliver. In these circumstances it is easy to understand why the Canadian producer is so keenly interested in reports of American policies that may be affecting the export sales of his product. Inability to deliver or delays in the date when delivery can be made, has helped to discourage wheat production, and by 1957 the acreage seeded to wheat in Canada was down 25 per cent from the 1949 peak. The comparable reduction in the United States from 1949 to 1957, under the impact of acreage restrictions, has been just over 40 per cent.

The second feature concerns the effects which the Canadian Wheat Board now exerts on world market prices for wheat. At the present time the bulk of the world's stocks of surplus wheat falls under the control of the governments of Canada and the United States, a paradoxical situation for two countries that are in the main devoted to the principle of free enterprise. If both countries were to return to a free market for wheat, there can be little doubt that prices would fall sharply. This is evident from the relation of prices to carryover presented in Chart 1. This chart indicates that whenever wheat stocks have become excessive in relation to current supplies under free market conditions in the past, wheat prices have fallen much more sharply than they have during the past few years. In fact, one of the two principal stock controlling countries, presumably Canada, has been acting as a price leader and setting selling prices on its product at levels significantly above those which would prevail in a free market. In this policy they have had the tacit consent of the United States government. For the latter, in setting the amount of its subsidies on wheat, does not attempt to undercut completely the Canadian Wheat Board price.[7] As long as this price is below a normal long-run equilibrium level, as it appears to be at the moment, it is unlikely to cause difficulties for the controlling authorities by inducing an expansion of output in other parts of the world. Nor do world wheat buyers have much cause for complaint about this price maintenance policy, since the Canadian wheat producer is currently supplying wheat for a lower net return than that received by any other wheat producer throughout the world.

[7] However, there is evidence that the United States engages in a good deal of price cutting in particular grades and markets. For example, an extra subsidy is offered on wheat flour, which has completely eliminated Canadian flour exports to many markets.

CHART I

EFFECTS OF CARRYOVER IN EXPORTING COUNTRIES ON PRICE OF
WHEAT, 1923-1939 AND 1946-1956

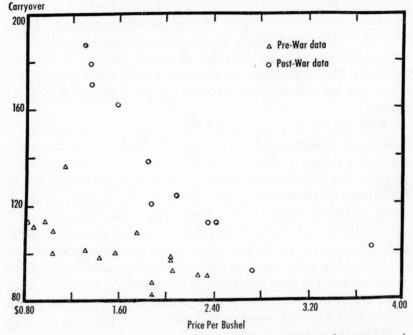

NOTE: Carryover at end of crop year for four major exporters plus new crop in
Canada and the United States expressed as per cent of a smoothed trend value of
exports plus domestic disappearance. This percentage value was then related to the
October price of No. 1 Northern Wheat at Fort William adjusted for change in
prices by the average price change shown in the Gross National Product.

VI

Let us now turn to an examination of the United States surplus
disposal program as it affects Canada. Although there had been some
earlier activity in the field, the surplus disposal of American farm
products did not reach large-scale proportions until after the passage
of the Agricultural Trade Development and Assistance Act of 1954
(Public Law 480). Under this law the government of the United
States is authorized to increase the export of American farm products
by any one or all of three different methods. First, surplus food
stocks can be given away to friendly foreign countries in need of
famine or disaster relief; donated to voluntary, nonprofit agencies
for distribution abroad; or given to such organizations as UNICEF

or the International Red Cross. Second, surplus farm products can be bartered for strategic materials or for materials or goods required for offshore constructions or in connection with foreign economic and military aid programs. Third, sales may be made for local currencies. The latter provision has in practice been the most important. Up to the end of December, 1957, agreements had been signed covering foreign currency sales to the value of $2,053 million. Some $852 million of this, or about 41 per cent of the total, was for the sale of wheat and wheat flour. An additional 6.6 per cent consisted of feed grains.[8]

Both the barter program and the foreign currency sales act to increase the market for American farm products and to undermine the export markets of Canada and other countries. Under the barter program the United States government arranges to supply surplus agricultural products to a private dealer in exchange for an undertaking to deliver certain specified materials within two years. The private dealer is then free to sell the agricultural products and purchase the materials on the best terms he can get. Formally, at least, the barter deal is arranged on the basis of competitive world market prices for both the farm products and the purchased materials. However, since many of the purchased materials end up in the supplemental stockpile, they represent net additions to the total world demand for the materials in question.[9] As such, they effectively support world prices for these materials. By the same token, they effectively increase competition in the world market for farm products. These increased sales cut into the regular commercial sales of all countries, including those of the United States. Canada has objected very strenuously to the barter program, apparently with some effect, for new contracts signed under the barter program in the six months ended December 31, 1957, have amounted to only $3 million, compared with contracts of $870 million in the three years preceding this period. One unfortunate by-product of the barter arrangements is the encouragement it gives to bilateral dealings and the bypassing of regular channels of international payments.

The effect of the foreign currency agreements on international

[8] Interagency Committee on Agricultural Surplus Disposal, *The Seventh Semiannual Report on Activities Carried on under Public Law 480, 83d Congress* (House Doc. 323, 85th Cong., 2d Sess., Washington, 1958), p. 3.

[9] See R. F. Mikesell, *Agricultural Surpluses and Export Policy* (Washington, 1958), pp. 14-15.

markets for farm products depends in part on what use is made of the currency received. If the currency is simply used by the United States to buy commodities that would otherwise have been purchased for dollars, the net effect is probably negligible. In fact, however, some 60 per cent of the total funds available to the United States under these agreements has been allocated to loans and grants for economic development. This has provided a strong incentive for the increased purchase of American farm products. In part, these will be bought in preference to the products of other countries. But in addition, the program undoubtedly leads to an increase in the total purchase of agricultural products by these countries. Without the additional aid received in this form these countries would still buy some wheat and other agricultural products. But they might buy a good deal less. Where such a genuine increase in purchases occurs there has been an effective disposal of some of the United States surplus.

Canada has objected strongly to a "tied sales" feature that has characterized some of the foreign currency agreements. Thus, Brazil, in return for being allowed to buy wheat for her own currency, was required to buy a certain volume of wheat for dollars for a stated period of years. Having been excluded from a major portion of Brazil's market because of the soft currency sales, Canadians feel that they should be allowed to compete on an even basis for whatever market remains.

VII

How has this surplus disposal program affected Canadian agriculture? To many Canadians, it has seemed almost obvious that the impact has been severe, especially on the producer of wheat. Consider the facts that have come to his attention. Both in terms of volume and value United States agricultural exports reached a new high in 1957. In contrast, Canadian agricultural exports were down over 10 per cent as compared with 1956. Between the crop years 1955-1956 and 1956-1957, United States wheat and wheat flour exports increased by over 200 million bushels. In the same period Canadian exports of wheat and wheat flour declined by 47 million bushels. This decline occurred in a year in which world wheat exports were at a record high. The implication to most Canadians is clear. The

United States surplus disposal program has cut heavily into sales of Canadian wheat. In the face of such evidence, American reassurances that their program is being administered in such a way as to avoid the disruption of normal commercial markets have fallen on deaf ears.

On closer examination the facts turn out to be more complex than most Canadians have been disposed to believe. In the main, the evidence suggests that the United States surplus disposal program has cut extensively into Canada's wheat and wheat flour markets in a number of Latin American countries such as Brazil, Bolivia, Columbia, Chile, and Peru, into some Middle Eastern markets such as Israel and Egypt, and into such Asian markets as India and Pakistan. It has not had a serious effect on Canada's sales to her traditional markets in Western Europe. There was some decline in Canadian sales to the United Kingdom in the crop year 1956-1957 and a corresponding increase in sales by the United States. Canadian grain officials contend that this shift from Canadian to American wheat was almost entirely the result of heavy purchases of wheat from United States barter contractors. In addition, the United States made sizable gains in sales of wheat to the Western European market in 1956-1957, and this may have been in part at the expense of potential Canadian sales. For many other countries the evidence is far from clear. Import requirements for wheat and wheat flour fluctuate so irregularly from year to year in many countries that it is difficult to reach any definite conclusions about what has been happening to Canadian sales. In some of these countries Canada may have lost some wheat sales or failed to make sales increases that would have been possible but for the United States surplus disposal program. In some instances, however, the evidence is very clear. For example, Canada has not sold any wheat or wheat flour at all to Brazil, Chile, or Egypt since July, 1954, whereas prior to that time her market in each of these three countries was substantial. Of the commodities other than wheat and wheat flour which have been the subject of surplus disposal, only feed grains and perhaps meat and dairy products are Canadian exports of any significance. Since for these products the amount exported under United States surplus disposal program has been much smaller than in the case of wheat and since Canadian exports of these products are not large, it is doubtful if there has been any serious loss of markets.

VIII

Canadians would feel happier about the United States surplus disposal program if they felt that it was in fact disposing of the surplus. Indeed, if such were the case they might be content to stand on the sidelines and cheer the United States on in the hope that, once the United States surplus had been disposed of, they might be able to sell their own surpluses at profitable prices. But up to the present it is far from clear that the program is, in fact, eliminating the surpluses. It is true that the Commodity Credit Corporation's investment in price-supported commodities declined by one billion dollars in the year ending in June, 1957. But stocks of wheat declined only about 125 million bushels and the crop now predicted for the current year may restore stocks to a new high. Moreover, under the United States price support formula any reduction in stocks leads automatically to an increase in the percentage of parity at which prices are supported, thus almost insuring that the reduction in the surplus will be short-lived.

While there may be disagreement about the wisdom of surplus disposal, about the facts of the surplus in the case of wheat there can be little doubt. At the end of the 1956-1957 crop year the carryover of wheat in the United States was the equivalent of nearly a year's production. In Canada the surplus problem is even more extreme; the wheat carryover on this same date amounted to more than one and a half times the output of a normal year. Despite her larger surplus, Canada has yet to show any signs of the panic which lies behind the United States disposal program.

About the source of the current wheat surplus there has also been some misunderstanding. Canadians have been prone to view the American surplus as the result of the price support program and nothing else. In contrast, their own surplus is attributed almost entirely to a period of exceptionally favorable weather. There is a large measure of truth in the latter contention though it may be that Canadians underestimate the extent to which improved agricultural techniques have been raising wheat yields.[10] In respect to the United States surplus there is need for more recognition in Canada of the fact that the period of high prices after the war and their brief renewal in the Korean War period led to an expansion of output which

[10] See W. M. Drumond and W. Mackenzie, *Progress and Prospects of Canadian Agriculture* (Ottawa, 1957), pp. 82-83.

would have created a difficult adjustment problem even in the absence of price supports in the United States. With the rapid recovery of European agricultural production and the persistence in many countries of agricultural protectionism some reduction in wheat output on this continent became inevitable. The acreage quotas imposed in the United States have helped produce some of this required reduction but their effectiveness has been limited by the way they have been administered. Moreover, the continuation of high support prices encourages the use of the best land for wheat production and the application of fertilizers and weed killers, all steps that increase the average yield per acre.

Whether the decline in acreage and output in the United States would have been more or less rapid under free market conditions is difficult to determine, but the rapid decline in wheat acreage following World War I suggests that a free market would have brought about a quicker adjustment.[11] It is true that the lower prices paid to Canadian wheat farmers have not produced any sharp reduction in acreage, but there are few practicable alternatives to wheat in the prairie provinces of western Canada. The continuation of the present price support program in the United States could easily delay the needed adjustment indefinitely. On the other hand, the problem might be solved by a more severe restriction of wheat acreage. The high domestic prices for wheat and feed grains that now exist in the United States not only encourage excessive production, but they also limit the use of these grains as feed for livestock and by supporting the price of all meat and dairy products prevent the general expansion in domestic demand that lower prices would induce. And lower domestic consumption means larger supplies for surplus disposal.

IX

Even in the absence of surplus disposal, current United States farm policy still affects Canadian agriculture in important ways. For some commodities the heavy subsidization involved in the price support program leads to increased competition in export markets. For other commodities the import quotas necessary to prevent other countries from taking advantage of the price support program reduce

[11] *Wheat Production*, Agriculture Information Bulletin No. 179, U. S. Department of Agriculture (Washington, 1958), pp. 12-14.

Canadian sales in the United States market. Let us look at each of these effects in turn.

Where American farm prices are supported at levels well above those prevailing on world markets, the extent of export competition depends on the export subsidy policy pursued by the United States government. The present policy is apparently one of selling on the export market at competitive world prices with a view to maintaining or restoring a "fair historical share" of the world market for United States agricultural exports.[12] If the historical share argument were taken seriously Canada might well argue that the United States has overshot the mark by a large margin in the case of wheat. The United States share of world wheat exports in 1956-1957 amounted to 45 per cent compared with 21 per cent in 1925-1929 and only 9 per cent in 1935-1939. In fact, of course, the fair historical share concept is virtually meaningless since changing techniques and market conditions will normally lead to changes in market shares.

Selling at world competitive prices apparently does not preclude co-operating with Canada in keeping world wheat prices well above the level that would prevail on an open market. It does not imply the dumping of all surplus supplies on the export market for whatever price they will bring. It is this very restraint in the export subsidization program that has created the need for surplus disposal. The disposal program represents an effort to eliminate the surpluses inherent in a price support program without at the same time disrupting world prices. It is perhaps worth noting that if the deficiency payment system advocated by some economists were substituted for the present price support program, the effects on world prices for many farm products might be severe. Such a system would involve a subsidy to domestic output without any control over exports unless the latter were explicitly added to the program.

It is perhaps natural that Canadian farmers should envy the generous subsidies received by their American cousins. However, only when these subsidies result in some direct reduction in Canadian farm income have they any real cause for complaint. Such an income loss could arise from a reduction in the Canadian share of the world market, or from a decline in world market prices, or from some combination of the two. Evidence was presented above that indicated some loss of Canadian wheat markets as a result of the surplus dis-

[12] Mikesell, *op. cit.*, pp. 36-37.

posal program. It seems likely that the heavily subsidized commercial sales of United States wheat have also caused some loss to Canadian farmers, mainly through exerting downward pressure on world wheat prices. Wheat prices have declined significantly in recent years and in real terms are now lower than at any time since 1933. However, it would be all but impossible to show any conclusive evidence of the extent to which the United States has been responsible for this decline.

The import quotas that the United States has imposed from time to time on Canadian farm products have undoubtedly caused some loss to Canadian farmers, but the best opinion seems to be that these effects have not been serious. Thus one recent study comments that import restraints

have been applied against relatively few Canadian products, quite sporadically and generally in a comparatively liberal manner. The quotas on coarse grains, for example, have been fair in relation to past trade and available supplies in Canada . . . . In a number of cases—for example, barley and oats—the restrictions were removed after a relatively short period of application. At present the restrictions which remain in force apply to wheat and flour, rye, dairy products, flaxseed, and linseed oil. It can be seen therefore that, apart from the grains, the United States restrictions have affected Canadian commodities which have been of relatively small importance in Canada's farm exports to the United States markets.[13]

Nevertheless, Canada has no real assurance that these quotas will not be applied or enforced more rigidly in the future. And the mere fact of their imposition, even though occasional, creates uncertainty in the minds of Canadian farmers and makes them reluctant to develop a market that may be suddenly shut off.

X

To sum up, thus far the effects of United States farm policy on Canadian agriculture have been serious but not catastrophic. The surplus disposal program has made serious inroads into or eliminated completely a number of smaller Canadian wheat markets but its overall effects have probably been less serious than Canadians have been disposed to believe. The extensive subsidies paid on commercial

[13] Irving Brecher and S. S. Reisman, *Canada-United States Economic Relations* (Ottawa, 1957), pp. 189-190.

exports have put downward pressure on wheat prices, but their effects have been limited by the willingness of the United States to co-operate with Canada in underpinning the world price of wheat. Canadian wheat producers are inclined to feel unjustly treated because they must compete on world markets with American farmers who receive a subsidy that amounts to more than half of their net return. But it is not entirely clear that the Canadian farmer would have been much better off in the complete absence of the American price support program. Under a system of free market prices the adjustment in wheat production on this continent might have taken place more quickly, but during the adjustment the effects on Canadian farm incomes might well have been severe. Moreover, past experience has shown that adjustments in agricultural production to changed market conditions sometimes take place very slowly if at all.

Apart from an occasional shout from the rooftops and some official representations in Washington, Canada has thus far taken little direct action to counteract these effects of American farm policy. Any extensive support to Canadian farmers in difficulties would be more burdensome for the Canadian government than it is to the United States Government. For example, on the basis of the average wheat production in the last five years, a subsidy of $1 a bushel would amount to about 2 per cent of Canada's national income compared with only about 0.3 per cent in the United States. It would be unwise, however, for the United States to rely on a presumed inability of Canada to meet a certain cost, as the St. Lawrence Seaway experience so clearly demonstrated. Canada has already initiated a surplus disposal policy of her own with a gift of 15 million bushels of wheat and flour to India, Pakistan, and Ceylon, and a $35 million credit to the Colombo Plan countries for the purchase of wheat and flour from Canada. If the concealed price-cutting implicit in the surplus disposal program should become more severe in its effects, Canada might decide to cut her export price sharply and bring the price cutting out into the open. Perhaps the threat of this can be depended on to keep the United States program within reasonable bounds.

5

The American Economic Impact on Quebec

Maurice Lamontagne

THE AMERICAN IMPACT on Quebec is not of recent origin. It first manifested itself mainly in political terms near the end of the first half of the nineteenth century. During the second half of that century, American influence became strictly economic and took the form of a massive emigration of French-Canadians to the United States. Finally, after World War I, the American economic impact on Quebec became more direct and more intensive, as growing amounts of United States capital were invested in resource industries which contributed to the development of new cities in rural Quebec. In many ways the United States influence and the local reaction to it were unique in Quebec. In order to understand the changing nature of that impact and the peculiar response it has received, it is necessary to study it in its historical and technological perspective.

Broadly speaking, modern economic development in Quebec as well as in the rest of Canada and in other Western countries took place in three distinct stages or periods. These periods may differ as to their timing from one country to the other but they largely coincide with important technological changes.

I. THE MERCANTILIST PERIOD

The first period of this modern age, which may be described as the mercantilist or pre-industrial era, came to an end in Canada about the middle of the nineteenth century. It was the period of the great commercial empires, when technology was based on wind, as the main source of power, on wood, as the most widely used raw material, and on navigation as the most important means of transportation.

Canadian resources were well adapted to that technological environment. Forest resources were abundant and the St. Lawrence Waterway provided easy access to a vast hinterland. Especially with the beginning of the Napoleonic wars, that period was one of intense prosperity in Canada. Economic activity was concentrated on such staple products as timber and furs and on shipbuilding. Exports of these products to the United Kingdom and, to a lesser extent, to the United States were greatly responsible for that prosperity and economic development. Quebec, with its resources and especially its navigation facilities, was then the geographical center of economic activity in Canada.

Lower Canada, as it was then called, was economically as well as politically dominated by British merchants and colonial officers and to a lesser extent by the Loyalists. The majority of French Canadians were living in the cities as laborers; they could not succeed easily in business because they never had any opportunity to accumulate capital and especially to develop trade connections. Some of them were earning a living from the fur trade or submarginal agriculture but, traditionally, they were not keen about farming and rural life.

In general, the higher clergy remained very faithful to Great Britain and the Crown because the British connection served to isolate the people from the influences of the French Revolution and its anticlericalism. The active participation of French Canadians in two wars against the United States was undoubtedly due in part to the attitude and the role of the clergy.

Gradually, however, a French Canadian "élite" developed. It was bound to become frustrated because it had no real outlets. Intellectual life was controlled by the Church; political life was controlled by the Colonial Office and it had no access to economic leadership. It led the fight for freedom on these three fronts but concentrated its efforts in the political field. At first, its objective was to get responsible government within the framework of British parliamentary institutions, but after several years of unsuccessful attempts to reach that goal, some of its principal spokesmen came to favor annexation by the United States. They had come to admire the American Revolution through the French Revolution.

Subjected to these two diverse influences, the French Canadian people liked neither the British nor Great Britain, but they were reluctant to break the British connection. On the other hand, although they did not favor annexation, they had a certain admiration for the American people; they certainly did not share with English-speaking Canadians the fear of the United States; they were much more afraid of Great Britain, which was the basis of rapprochement with the Americans.

On the whole, during this mercantilist period, the American impact on Quebec was slight and mainly political in character. It is important, however, in explaining the kind of reaction created by the much deeper influence that the United States was to have in Quebec later on.

II. THE FIRST PERIOD OF INDUSTRIALIZATION (1850-1920)

As is well known, the Industrial Revolution, which first developed in Great Britain, was based on coal, steel, and railroads. The new technology had very favorable effects in Western Europe and in the United States, but quite an unfavorable impact on Canada. As a result of that technological revolution, Great Britain adopted free trade and later on the United States decided to move toward greater protection. These two decisions meant a decisive blow for Canadian export trade. Moreover, the shipbuilding industry was wiped out, lumber lost its predominance as a raw material, and the St. Lawrence River ceased to have its traditional commercial importance. Finally, Canada did not then have the resources required by the new technology suitably located in sufficient quantities.

The Canadian Confederation was set up, after prolonged discussions, as a defensive move against the American menace but also as a political structure required by the former colonies to overcome the unfavorable impact of the Industrial Revolution and to adjust their production and transportation facilities to the new technology. The objective of the Fathers of Confederation was to extend and unify the Canadian territory and to create, as the Americans were doing, a western economic frontier which would stimulate industrial development in the East. That objective, however, was not fully met until 1896, in spite of the National Policy initiated by Sir John A. Macdonald in 1879 and designed to protect manufacturing industries.

Until the end of the nineteenth century, economic development in Canada was rather slow because of the unfavorable technological climate and the long world depression. However, railway construction contributed greatly to create a domestic market for steel and a more specialized agriculture in the East, and helped to develop a growing market for consumer goods. These two factors, together with the National Policy, were mainly responsible for the establishment in Canada of the manufacturing industries resulting from the new technological age.

However, the real impetus to industrial expansion came at the end of the century when world economic conditions and the discovery of Red Fyfe wheat led to the opening up of the West. Wheat very quickly became the main Canadian export and the dynamic factor of development. The Prairies were populated very rapidly and were devoted almost exclusively to wheat production. Thus, a vast market was created for the industrial products of the East and very important complementary relationships were developed between these two economic regions. Moreover, wheat exports from the Prairies helped to reduce Canada's trade deficit and to compensate for the imports needed by the more industrialized provinces.

During the latter part of that first period of industrialization, therefore, the Canadian economy had succeeded, despite the technological climate of the times, in achieving balance, though precarious, because of the risks involved in wheat production; but this undoubtedly was the most satisfactory arrangement under the circumstances. The so-called North Atlantic triangle had been developed. In 1900, for instance, 60 per cent of our imports came from the United States and 24 per cent from the United Kingdom; 13.5 per cent of total foreign capital invested in Canada was American and 85 per cent was British; 34 per cent of our exports were going to the United States and 57 per cent to the United Kingdom.

This period witnessed a drastic change in the geographical orientation of Canadian industrial development. Location factors became greatly favorable to Ontario. Quebec lost the geographical advantages it had enjoyed during the previous period. Ontario was at the center of the Canadian market and had easy access to those areas in the United States which were producing coal and iron ore. These geographical factors meant, when the National Policy was initiated, that Ontario was the ideal location for the new manufacturing industries and especially for heavy industries.

Quebec was left with one favorable location factor, which was an abundant and therefore cheap labor supply resulting from a rapid natural increase in population. Labor-using and light-consumer-goods industries, such as textiles, boots and shoes, and tobacco were induced to locate in Quebec because they could not afford to pay high wages. However, the development of these industries was too slow to provide sufficient employment opportunities for a rapidly growing labor force at a time when older industries and trades were disappearing.

The inadequacy of the demand for labor in Quebec was especially evident during the second half of the nineteenth century. As we have seen earlier, French Canadians had no deeply rooted rural tradition, but many of them were forced to leave the cities and to become farmers. However, the area of easily accessible arable land was limited in Quebec, and this rural movement could not solve the problem of surplus population in a depressed economy. Other French Canadians left Quebec for Saskatchewan and for Manitoba, which had become the center of the fur trade. But the great bulk of French-Canadian emigrants went to the United States, especially to New England, where the textile industry was expanding rapidly. It has been estimated that more than 500,000 people participated in this huge migration movement during these decades. These French Canadians would undoubtedly have preferred to stay in Quebec but their emigration to the United States was certainly made easier because of the admiration and the good feelings they and their "élite" had developed for that country during the first half of the century. Though most of them preserved their language and religion, they adjusted themselves very rapidly to the American environment, and they showed a certain contempt for their country of origin, which was so closely associated in their minds with their former poverty and misery. This massive emigration helped to intensify the good relations already existing between the United States and French Canada.

During the pre-industrial era, the American Revolution had exercised a distinct political impact on Quebec, especially on the French-Canadian "élite," which inspired the annexation movement. During the first period of industrialization, the American impact had been indirect but more economic. The dream of political annexation had been replaced by massive emigration. As a consequence of the most unfavorable effects that the Industrial Revolution had in Quebec, the

United States and especially New England had become a very important labor market for French Canadians, at least until 1900.

In the meantime, responsible government had been granted to the colonies in British North America and, especially after Confederation, French Canadians had as much control over their political life as they could expect to have in a federal state. However, the situation in the economic field was quite different. English-speaking Canadians really dominated the scene, and to the extent that foreign capital was supplied to promote industrial development, it was largely of British origin. This fact, together with a growing wage differential between Ontario and Quebec, which was due largely to differences in the industrial structure of the two provinces and to the relative abundance of labor in Quebec, but which was not interpreted in those terms, led to intensified ill-feelings against the British and English-speaking Canadians in French Canada. These feelings were further strengthened by the Riel incident, the school question as it arose outside Quebec, our participation in two so-called imperialistic wars, the conscription issue, and the frequent statements made in some English-speaking circles which implied that Quebec was a backward region and a priest-ridden province.

III. THE SECOND PERIOD OF INDUSTRIALIZATION (1920-1958)

The fact that the twentieth century has witnessed a second industrial revolution based on new technological factors and new products has not received sufficient attention. At the beginning of the century, but especially after World War I, water, oil, and gas became new sources of energy; great progress was made in the long-distance transmission of electricity; substitutes for steel, such as nickel, copper, and aluminium, were more widely used; the motor car and the airplane, radio, and television revolutionized transportation and communications; wood gained a new importance in the fabrication of paper and plastics; and the electric appliance and chemical industries were rapidly developed. While the new technology did not destroy the old one, it resulted in a drastic re-direction of economic development in the world. The new technological factors had an unfavorable impact on Western Europe but greatly favored North America and especially Canada.

Great Britain could not adapt herself easily to the new technological environment, and the United States emerged as the dominant force leading the world into this second industrial revolution. The Americans had developed mass-production techniques; they had the capital and the know-how, but they did not have in sufficient quantities some of the resources required by the new technology. Canada, on the other hand, had these resources in abundance and a protected domestic market for the new products, but lacked capital and technical knowledge. These basic factors largely determined the course of Canadian economic history, especially after World War I; this period was characterized by the opening up of our northern economic frontier, rapid industrial development, and closer integration to the North American continental economy.

The process of economic integration to the United States was evident during the first two decades of the present century but, as statistics on trade and foreign investments indicate, it became still more rapid after 1920. In that year 68.9 per cent of our imports and 43.7 per cent of total foreign capital invested in Canada came from the United States, and 43.8 per cent of our exports were sold on the American market. In 1955, 73.3 per cent of total imports and 76.3 per cent of foreign capital originated from the United States, which bought 59.8 per cent of total Canadian exports.

The integration of the Canadian economy to that of the United States was accomplished in three distinct stages. First, the United States became the chief source of supply for Canadian imports at the beginning of the century. Railways and road transportation greatly contributed to the development of a continental economy and to intensified trade relations between the two countries. American advertising in Canada, through the new media of mass communication, created a demand in our country for American products. For these reasons, and because United States producers were the most efficient if not the only suppliers of the products developed by the new technology, Canadian imports of machinery, equipment, and durable consumer goods from the United States increased rapidly and constituted the great bulk of our purchases abroad.

During the second stage, after World War I, the United States became our main source of foreign capital. American capital was invested in ever-increasing amounts in Canada, either to supply the Canadian and Commonwealth protected markets with the manufactured products of the new technological age or to develop resource industries in Canada and to supply the American market with the raw materials and semifinished products needed by United States producers.

During the third stage, especially after World War II, Western Europe and the Sterling Area experienced balance of payments difficulties which were directly connected with the impact of the second industrial revolution, and the United States had to rely more and more on foreign sources of supply for raw materials. As a consequence, the Canadian export trade was redirected and the American market became the main outlet for our products. This third stage completed the process of integration of the North American economy. The opening up of the Canadian West had tended to dissociate the economies of the two countries; the opening up of the North, curiously enough, was linking them together more closely than ever before.

During the last three decades at least, the American economic impact on Canada has been growing; it is likely to remain very great in the future, especially if Canadians want to continue to enjoy rapid economic development and a high standard of living, unless free trade is gradually established between the nations of the Western World.

This economic impact has not had a uniform regional incidence. It has been relatively small in the Maritime provinces and it is comparatively new, but growing, in western Canada and in British Columbia. It was felt earlier and most heavily in Ontario; it appeared later in Quebec and was more concentrated in the sector of resource industries.

Ontario is probably the Canadian province which is most dependent on American investment and imports from the United States, while the bulk of its production is sold on the domestic market. When American industries decided to establish subsidiaries in Canada to manufacture the products of the new technology, such as automobiles, electrical appliances, and other semidurable goods, they selected Ontario in most cases, mainly because of its geographical location. American investments were also important in the sector of resource industries, but they were not predominant.

While the industrialization movement in Ontario during the first industrial revolution had been relatively rapid and based on heavy industries, in Quebec it had been relatively slow and limited to soft consumer-good industries. The second industrial revolution, however, had a very favorable impact on Quebec, chiefly because of its water, forest, and mining resources.

After 1920 the old manufacturing industries, dependent on Canadian capital and cheap labor, expanded slowly. Only a few new ones, such as the chemical industry and synthetic textiles, were developed with the assistance of American capital. The Du Pont Company of Canada, Canadian Celanese, and Canadian Chemical played an important role in this new development.

The most spectacular expansion, however, took place in the sector of resource industries. The pulp and paper industry and the primary aluminum industry, together with hydro-power developments, inaugurated the new industrial era in Quebec. In each case, American capital and the United States market dominated the scene. The Aluminium Company of Canada, Canadian International Paper, Quebec North Shore, Ontario Paper, and the Brown Company illustrate this fact.

For a long period the mining industry was limited to the extraction of asbestos in the Eastern Townships. The Canadian Johns-Manville Company, a subsidiary of the American company, is now the biggest asbestos producer. The great period of expansion of the mining industry started only during the great depression of the thirties. The Abitibi region was the first center of this new activity which resulted from the extension of mining operations in Northern Ontario to the Quebec gold belt and was financed largely from Toronto. After World War II the mining industry expanded rapidly; mining operations were further extended to the North-East and the exploitation of huge iron ore deposits was initiated. This new development, which marked the opening up of Northern Quebec was undertaken by American capital to meet the needs of the United States market.

The rapid expansion of the tourist trade, which the motor car greatly facilitated after 1920, is another important aspect of the American economic impact on Quebec. In fact, several economic regions in the province, especially on the south shore of the St. Lawrence River, depend for their prosperity on the flow of American tourists.

IV. CANADIAN REACTION TO AMERICAN INVESTMENT IN
ONTARIO AND QUEBEC

Over the years, the growing American economic impact on the
two largest Canadian provinces has led to two quite different reactions. In Ontario the fear has been expressed that Canadians were
losing the control over their economic and cultural life and it has been
accompanied by growing anti-American feelings. United States participation in Canadian industrial expansion has produced a more
rapid development and a higher standard of living but also, as a by-
product, a greater sense of inferiority and frustration, a growing opposition to closer economic integration which could weaken national
identity. In Quebec, on the contrary, American economic influence
has been welcomed and the fear of the dangers involved, if it existed
at all, has seldom been expressed until recently. Several factors account for these two different reactions.

In Ontario, anti-American feelings are not new; they have their
roots in the American Revolution, while pro-British feelings in the
past have always been strong. Moreover, English-speaking Canadians share their language and religion with the Americans, which
means that they are directly exposed to what is viewed as the danger
of "americanization." On the other hand, in earlier periods, English-
speaking businessmen had been accustomed, with the assistance of
British capital, to dominate Canadian economic development. When
United States capital started to flow into Canada, followed by American managers, this meant a new and strong competition and Canadians lost in part the initiative and influence they formerly had. This
new threat was, of course, a cause of resentment. Finally, American
investment in Ontario certainly contributed to more rapid economic
expansion but it did not really initiate a new period of industrialization. Even during the latter part of the nineteenth century, Ontario
had developed rapidly and there was no perceptible wage differential
between old and new industries when American capital started to pour
in. The population, therefore, was already accustomed to a relatively
high standard of living and hardly noticed the special benefits derived
from the flow of American capital.

In Quebec the situation was quite different. Pro-American feelings had been cultivated since the early part of the nineteenth century.
Massive emigration to the United States had intensified the links be-

tween the two people. The rising flow of American tourists after 1920 had a similar result. On the other hand, anti-British feelings were deeply rooted and were extended to English-speaking Canadians, who were accused of being more British than Canadian. As a result of the ethnic difficulties which had developed during the earlier period, isolationism and provincial autonomy became the dominant theme of French-Canadian nationalism, under the inspiration of Abbé Groulx, after World War I. For the majority of French-Canadians, the most immediate danger did not come from the United States but from English-speaking Canada.

There were, especially in the thirties, both resentment and anxiety in Quebec about the fact that English-speaking businessmen and managers were controlling the economy of the province. It is interesting to note that the same grievances expressed by French-Canadians against English-Canadians on that subject are now made by the latter against the Americans. French-Canadians, however, never had any really effective control over their economic life; their dominant fear was to lose the control over their political life through increasing centralization of powers by the federal government, which ultimately could mean cultural assimilation.

Moreover, the significance of the American economic impact was quite different in Quebec from what it was in Ontario. In the first place, the flow of American investment did not really affect the relative importance of French-speaking businessmen in Quebec because they had never been in a dominant position in the past. It was an alternative only to what were already considered in Quebec as "foreign" sources of capital.

In the second place, the flow of American investment was directly related to rapid industrial expansion in Quebec and the establishment of a new type of industries based on the utilization of abundant natural resources rather than cheap labor, as was the case with the old consumer-goods industries developed during an earlier period with Canadian and British capital. American investment became associated with high wages and increased employment opportunities on a more decentralized basis. These results were considered as being very desirable and contributed greatly toward the creation of a favorable climate for American capital in Quebec.

Recently, however, there has been some indication that this situa-

tion may change. For the time being, the signs of a change in out-
look are restricted to a small "élite."

The new generation of French-Canadian intellectuals does not
show any real anti-British feelings. It has developed close cultural
relationships with France, and it is very conscious of the danger of
"americanization" to which even French-Canadians are directly exposed. It is using more and more the anti-American themes which
have become so popular in other parts of the world in the postwar
period. It is too early yet, however, to see in what direction this new
anti-American trend will move and to what extent it will influence the
French-Canadian people itself. It may develop into a more positive
and healthy Canadianism or into a rather negative and narrow
French-Canadian nationalism. The attitude that English-speaking
Canadians will take from now on toward French-Canadian culture
and its role outside Quebec will undoubtedly have a great influence
on the orientation that will be followed in Quebec.

6

The Flow of United States Investment Funds into Canada Since World War II*

Irving Brecher

Canadian-american problems have as long a history as the Canaian economy itself. Over the years since Confederation, and even before, many mutually relevant economic, social, and political issues have captured public attention on both sides of the border. Indeed, it could hardly have been otherwise—given the facts of geographic proximity, common cultural heritage, and extensive trade and migration between the two countries.

From this perspective, United States investment in Canada takes its place as only one of many topics continuously emerging in Canadian-American discussion. Nor can such investment be logically viewed in isolation; it is closely intertwined with commercial, political, and other considerations. Moreover, this particular issue is not a new one; it is a hardy perennial with roots going well back into the period between the two World Wars.

And yet, while recognizing these truths, one cannot avoid the

*Between 1945 and 1956 Canadian long-term investments abroad increased from about $2 billion to nearly $4.5 billion. When allowance is made for the equity of nonresident owners of Canadian corporations, the 1956 figure totals approximately $3.7 billion. This, in turn, amounts to more than $225 per capita, as compared with some $265 per capita for long-term investments held outside the United States by residents of that country. At the end of 1956 residents of Canada held over $2 billion worth of long-term investments in the United States. Dominion Bureau of Statistics, *The Canadian Balance of International Payments, 1957, and International Investment Position* (Ottawa, 1958), p. 45.

Such figures underscore the fact that the post-World War II flow of investment funds between Canada and the United States has been much more than a one-way movement from the United States to Canada. But while recognizing the quantitative importance of the Canadian outflow, this paper confines itself to a treatment of United States investments in the Canadian economy. To some extent, this procedure represents an arbitrary decision to place workable limits on the scope of discussion. The prime reason for the "Canadian inflow" approach, however, is that United States investment has been a far more significant element in Canadian economic activity than has Canadian investment in the United States; and that, in consequence, it is the former which has aroused the greater interest and the deeper concern.

judgment that for vigor, pervasiveness, and speed of development, the current concern over the "United States investment" question represents something unique in Canadian-American relations. In both countries the past few years have witnessed an unprecedented outpouring of varied, often conflicting, private and public views on this question. The intensity of debate has, in part, been a natural reflection of Canada's growing stature in North American and world affairs, and of an increasing popular distaste for those aspects of foreign ownership and control which can be construed as economic apron strings. No less pertinent are the striking dimensions and rate of growth of present United States investment in Canadian industry which, together with uneasiness and uncertainty about its underlying implications for the Canadian economy, have undoubtedly helped to make this a focal point for more general frustrations and dissatisfactions. At the same time, profound concern has developed lest these attitudes lead to extreme measures which might seriously reduce the attractiveness of foreign capital investment in Canada.

This paper sets out to perform a modest task. It proceeds on the assumption that the essential requisites for sound policy in this field are Canadian-American harmony and a broad grasp of basic information on the meaning and effects of United States investment in Canada. Accordingly, the discussion will incorporate the following elements: first, a summary of the quantitative facts on United States investment; second, a review of the major "problem areas" as seen by Canadian observers; third, an outline of available findings on the real significance of United States investment for Canadian welfare; fourth, suggestions for further research designed to promote increased understanding of the forces at work in the investment sphere; and finally, some reflections on alternative public-policy approaches to United States investment in Canadian industry.

I. EXTENT OF UNITED STATES INVESTMENT IN CANADA

It is well known that investment in general, and long-term foreign capital in particular, have traditionally ranked among the main determinants of Canadian economic growth. The bulk of the external capital has originated in the United States and Western Europe. It has, therefore, by no means been exclusively a matter of American flows. The focus of current Canadian attention is, nevertheless, on the United States, and the reasons are not far to seek. The fact is that an extraordinarily high proportion of the post-World War II increase in foreign capital has come from the United States, and that in large measure it has taken the form of direct investment in the most dynamic sectors of Canadian industry.[1]

The following factual observations highlight the nature and dimensions of foreign investment in Canada:[2]

1. Between 1900 and 1957 *total long-term foreign capital* invested in Canada increased from $1.2 billion to $17.1 billion.

2. More than *half of this increase* has occurred since the end of World War II, with most of the postwar rise coming after 1948.

3. About *three-fourths* of all foreign capital invested in Canada is now *held in the United States*. This is in sharp contrast with the pattern immediately after World War I, when 60 per cent of foreign capital was held in the United Kingdom.

4. At present *direct investment*, 83 per cent of it American, accounts for *57 per cent of total foreign investment*, as contrasted with earlier years when *portfolio investment* was the dominant form.

5. Nonresidents controlled 30 per cent of Canada's *industrial sector* at the beginning of 1956, as compared with 17 per cent in 1926. During the same period the United States' share increased from 16 per cent to 26 per cent.[3]

[1] "Direct investment refers to the investment in or retention of earnings by concerns which are effectively controlled by non-residents. These include all concerns in Canada which are known to have 50 per cent or more of their voting stock held in one country outside Canada. In addition, in a few instances, concerns are included where it is known that effective control is held by a parent firm with less than 50 per cent of the stock. In effect this category includes all known cases of unincorporated branches of foreign companies in Canada and all wholly-owned subsidiaries, together with a number of concerns with a parent company outside of Canada which holds less than all of the capital stock. In addition, there is a relatively small number of Canadian companies included in cases where more than one-half of their capital stock is owned in a single country outside of Canada where there is no parent concern. These exceptional cases are confined to instances where control is believed to rest with non-residents." Royal Commission on Canada's Economic Prospects, *Final Report* (Ottawa, 1957), p. 380 n. It will be seen later that "statistical" or potential control does not necessarily imply actual control over corporate decision-making.

[2] All foreign-investment figures are derived from three publications: D.B.S., *Canada's International Investment Position, 1926-1954* (Ottawa, 1956); Irving Brecher and S. S. Reisman, *Canada-United States Economic Relations* (Royal Commission on Canada's Economic Prospects, Ottawa, 1957); D.B.S., *The Canadian Balance of International Payments, 1957, and International Investment Position.*

[3] In industry generally and in manufacturing, the United States control ratio

6. At the beginning of 1956 nonresidents controlled 57 per cent of the total investment in Canadian *manufacturing,* and 66 per cent of the total in *mining, smelting, and petroleum exploration and development.* In 1926 the control ratios were 35 per cent and 38 per cent, respectively. The United States share for these two sectors amounted to 47 per cent and 64 per cent, respectively, in 1955 as compared with 30 per cent and 32 per cent in 1926. (See Appendix Tables 9, 10, and 11 for additional data on the above points.)

7. In a number of *important Canadian industries*—including oil and gas, nickel, aluminum, asbestos, iron ore, automobiles, electrical apparatus, rubber, and chemicals—a few enterprises owned and controlled by United States residents account for a preponderant share of total investment, output, and employment.

8. In 1956 and 1957 approximately *two-fifths of net capital formation* in Canada was directly financed by nonresidents.[4]

It is apparent that the scope and pattern of foreign investment in Canada are too complex to be described with full precision by any single summary statement. Perhaps the best generalization is that it is "large, growing rapidly, mainly American, and heavily concentrated in the resource and manufacturing industries."[5]

---

rose less on a relative basis than the control ratios for nonresident investment as a whole. This, of course, is not inconsistent with the fact of enormous increase in United States investment in Canadian industry. Indeed, the period 1926-1956 shows a decline in the ratio of foreign-owned investment to total investment in domestic industry; this despite a large-scale increase in the United States ratio over the same period. It is on the "control" side that in certain instances the nonresident share as a whole rose more rapidly than the United States share in particular.

[4] This estimate comprises the inflow of long-term foreign capital plus the nonresident share of retained earnings of foreign-controlled enterprises in Canada. Alternatively, the role of foreign financing can be gauged by estimating the extent to which Canada has, on balance, drawn on the resources of other countries for the savings available for investment in Canada. The latter approach entails adding Canada's balance on current international account to the excess of undistributed profits on foreign direct investments in Canada over undistributed profits accruing to Canadian residents from direct investments abroad. On this net basis, it has been estimated that over the years 1946-1954 Canadian savings were large enough to finance all but 6 per cent of the country's net capital formation. The great contrast between this ratio and the one cited above stems from the different time periods covered by the two figures, and from the fact that a substantial portion of Canadian savings was invested abroad. D.B.S., *Canada's International Investment Position, 1926-54,* pp. 45-47; and D.B.S., *The Canadian Balance of International Payments, 1957,* pp. 30, 31.

[5] Brecher and Reisman, *op. cit.,* p. 156.

II. PROBLEM AREAS

Confronted with such striking facts, it is quite natural that Canadians should be giving voice to serious concern over the future course of Canada's economic development. Nor is it surprising that this concern should be aggravated by an all-too-frequent American reluctance to gain an understanding of the Canadian point of view.[6] In this context it is not enough to dismiss Canadian complaints as groundless or imaginary. On careful analysis this may turn out to be the case for some, but not for others. In any event, all of the problems are subjectively real for those who raise them; and only through sympathetic inquiry can objective truth be identified and constructive solutions found.[7]

1. General Considerations. Underlying much of the current Canadian discussion "there seems to be a deep, though intangible, sense of disquiet over the social and political implications of large-scale and continuing United States ownership and control of Canadian industry."[8] Apparently, the fundamental question here is whether Canada's social vitality is weakened and its political sovereignty compromised by the fact that Americans own an important part of its basic industry and resources and are therefore in a position to make key decisions affecting its operation and development. Very much to the fore is a growing national pride and an accompanying anxiety lest irreparable damage be done to Canadian independence of thought and action.

A second major source of Canadian concern involves the division of financial returns accruing from the country's economic development. Nonresident investors, particularly Americans, have long shared extensively in the monetary fruits of Canadian growth. This

[6] "The United States and its citizens have frequently adopted a patronizing assumption that Canada, like a poor relation, would remain at our beck and call, and that no matter what the provocation, Canadians would not object to any step we might take. This lack of interest, this ignorance of the Canadian heritage and Canadian problems, and this patronizing air have been displayed by the people, the press, and the Government of the United States . . . . Sources such as these underlie much of the irritation and misunderstanding between the United States and Canada." *Report of the Special Study Mission to Canada Comprising Hon. Brooks Hays, Arkansas, [and] Hon. Frank M. Coffin, Maine, of the Committee on Foreign Affairs,* 85th Cong., 2d Sess., House Report No. 1766, pp. 3-4.

[7] This is not to suggest that all "investment" issues can be conclusively resolved, but rather that maximum results will be achieved by viewing them in the light of reason and common sense.

[8] Brecher and Reisman, *op. cit.,* p. 152.

fact disturbs those Canadians who believe that the preponderant gains rightfully belong to the residents of the country whose natural resources provide the essential ingredient for economic expansion. And this attitude of concern is reinforced by the widespread conviction that the future points to the maintenance, and possibly even enlargement, of the present American share.

2. *Stability, Efficiency, and Growth.* There are, in the third place, a number of Canadian grievances relating to the alleged general effects of United States investment on Canadian stability, efficiency, and growth. The "stability" argument has two important facets. On the one hand, it is claimed that a massive withdrawal, or a suddenly halted inflow, of American capital would have serious adverse repercussions on Canadian levels of income and employment. On the other hand, it is widely held that domestic control of inflation is greatly impeded by virtue of the access which United States-owned companies have either directly to their parents' funds or more generally to the capital market in the United States.[9] In both these ways, it is argued, the Canadian economy is rendered more open, and therefore more "cycle-sensitive," than it would otherwise be.[10]

As regards economic efficiency, many Canadians have expressed special concern over the dominant position of large United States-controlled firms in important Canadian industries:

The influence which foreign-controlled concerns exert in some industries may be greater than the percentages which the amount of foreign capital investment in these industries might imply at first glance. This is because, in Canada, a relatively few large firms tend to predominate in many industries; and the influence which they exert in such industries may be pervasive and compelling. If these few large firms, or a majority of them, are controlled by nonresidents of Canada, it may follow that the foreign capital invested in the industry, because of the way in which it is concentrated,

[9] "Not only do the executives of Canadian branches of United States corporations have this alternative open to them in an unusual degree; they may also be less convinced than their counterparts in Canadian-controlled companies of the appropriateness of the policies being followed." F. A. Knox, "United States Capital Investment in Canada," *Papers and Proceedings of the American Economic Association*, XLVII (1957), 608. In the same connection, see C. D. Blyth and and E. B. Carty, "Non-Resident Ownership of Canadian Industry," *Canadian Journal of Economics and Political Science*, XXII (1956), 460.

[10] It is further alleged that some American companies operating in Canada aggravate business fluctuations by making frequent short-run shifts in the allocation of production and exports within the international enterprise. This issue will be elaborated in subsequent discussion of company policies and practices.

in fact dominates or at least influences greatly the operations and the general conduct of the entire industry.[11]

Implicit in this approach is the fear that the great size of many American-owned firms, in relation to both the size of resident-owned companies and the size of the domestic market, increases the extent to which the Canadian economy is permeated by "monopoly." This sense of anxiety is strengthened by the demonstrable fact of relatively greater concentration in Canadian than American industry.[12]

In the sphere of growth it is often argued that over the long run United States investment might impose a heavy transfer burden on the Canadian economy. In balance-of-payments terms the expanded role of flexible dividends relative to rigid interest payments is conceded to have improved Canada's position vis à vis the strains which might be generated in a business recession. Against this advantage, however, is set the transfer disadvantage inherent in the prospects for growing profit flows out of the Canadian economy. The conclusion is accordingly reached that "the balance-of-payments debits arising from foreign investments in Canadian industry will continue longer and will probably be higher because of the extent to which such investments are controlled as well as owned outside the country."[13]

3. *Company Policies and Practices.* Perhaps the most widely aired complaints are those associated with the specific policies and practices of American enterprises operating in Canada. Over a broad cross-section of Canadian opinion the behavior of these companies has been held to exert, or to carry the potential of, serious adverse effects on the Canadian economy. And in periods of recession there are added Canadian fears that economic contraction opens up wider possibilities for injurious corporate practices.

Here the overriding consideration would appear to be the alleged fact of both formal and actual control residing abroad. For the great majority of these enterprises, the United States parent or the principal American shareholders are deemed not only to have ultimate stock-voting authority but to make the basic operating de-

[11] Royal Commission on Canada's Economic Prospects, *Preliminary Report* (Ottawa, 1956), pp. 87-88.
[12] See Gideon Rosenbluth, *Concentration in Canadian Manufacturing Industries* (Princeton, 1957), chap. iv.
[13] Knox, *op cit.*, p. 608.

cisions as well.   In this setting, it is argued, policies are formulated and actions taken which are inimical to the best economic interests of Canada.

One such instance is provided by personnel policy.   The complaint is typically made that few Canadians find a place on the boards of directors or at the senior management level of United States-controlled companies.[14]   This is taken as disturbing evidence of both the completeness of foreign control and the virtual absence of the "Canadian viewpoint" in company decisions.

The field of research represents another important area of Canadian concern.   American technology and research are generally acknowledged to confer enormous benefits on the Canadian economy. At the same time, it is contended that little if any significant research is done at the Canadian end of United States-company operations; and that the long-run effect of this extensive borrowing process must be to limit opportunities for the employment of technical and professional skills in Canada, and to deprive Canada of that initiative and resourcefulness so vital to industrial progress.

Concern has also been expressed over the decisions taken by United States enterprises regarding the location and expansion of industrial facilities in Canada.   It is pointed out, in this connection, that American owners are naturally interested in protecting the value of investments already made in facilities in the United States; and further that they can be expected, as a matter of national preference, to favor American over Canadian location and expansion.   The consequence, it is reasoned, is that Canadian industrial development tends to proceed at least in some directions at a slower pace than would prevail under circumstances of more widespread Canadian ownership and control.   The retarded state of advanced manufacturing in Canada is held to be a direct reflection of this relationship between United States control and Canadian growth.

In no area has Canadian concern been more articulate than with respect to the marketing and purchasing policies of American enterprises operating in Canada.   On the marketing side, the general rule is alleged to be one of restraint against export sales by the Canadian subsidiary, such restraint taking the form of either outright prohibi-

[14] See, for example, the address of Dr. G. E. Hall, President of the University of Western Ontario, "Taking Canada for Granted," at the Boston Conference on Distribution, 1955, as quoted in *The Financial Post*, Toronto, Oct. 22, 1955, p. 25.

tion or confinement of sales to particular overseas markets. Along with plant-location policy, this practice is thought to have an important bearing on Canada's limited exports of highly processed goods. Hardly less pervasive, it is claimed, is the parental policy of requiring that the subsidiary, regardless of price, purchase its supplies of materials and equipment in the United States—either from the parent itself or from the parent's suppliers. A double impact is thereby felt: the subsidiary's costs of production are artificially raised; and the supply-geared activities of Canadian business are unduly discouraged.

Still another aspect of company practice relates to the rate of resource development. In this context, Canadians have often pointed to the danger that an American company developing a resource in a number of countries including Canada may postpone the Canadian production in favor of greater utilization of United States reserves or politically-vulnerable overseas holdings. Under Canadian control, by contrast, the rate of development would be governed not by considerations of global policy but by the economic merits of the Canadian project. The result might well be speedier exploitation of the resource in Canadian than in American hands.

Then, too, Canadians have expressed doubts as to the price policies followed by United States firms operating in Canada. In particular, attention has been drawn to the pricing of goods produced mainly for the export market, and to the pricing of transactions conducted within the international company. The disadvantage attributed to export pricing is that such an enterprise is unusually susceptible to low-price pressures emanating from private and public groups within the United States; to yield to such pressures is, of course, to reduce the financial returns of the industry. As for intracompany pricing, the grievance is that the American parent, keen on showing high profits for its United States operation, often prices the subsidiary's products below "market level" and in this way adversely affects the latter's profit position.

There is, furthermore, the alleged problem of production instability stemming from the ups and downs of the business cycle. In the downswing phase, it is argued, the American company is likely to curtail its foreign operations before its domestic activities; in some cases decisions may also be taken to curb imports from the Canadian subsidiary into the American market and to readjust high inventories of United States-produced goods through increased exports into the marketing channels of the subsidiary. To that extent, the subsidiary will bear a heavier burden of cyclical decline than it would if owned by Canadian interests. During inflation, on the other hand, reverse pressures are held to be likely, with a resultant accentuation of excess demand; and the relaxation of these pressures in time of cyclical contraction would, without more, be sufficient to accelerate the downward movement in Canadian economic activity.

Reference should, finally, be made to three other issues which have provoked critical comment in Canada.[15] One relates to the influence of tariff policy: where the parent company enjoys American tariff protection against its Canadian subsidiary's products, it may strongly discourage the subsidiary from joining in any Canadian-sponsored effort to achieve a reduced United States tariff. Secondly, many Canadians have been disturbed over what they regard as a general tendency of American-owned Canadian subsidiaries to "pull less than their full weight" in the matter of contributing to the support of Canadian education, charitable institutions, and other areas of social welfare; this performance allegedly reflecting the indiscriminate extension to Canada of a widespread parental policy of limited participation in United States welfare projects.[16] More recently, substantial Canadian concern has arisen over the possibility that an American parent, under legislative or policy restraint of the United States government, would impose limits on the freedom of action of its Canadian subsidiary. Indeed, in terms of the intensity of Canadian reaction, such restrictions appear to be among the most serious of all.[17]

[15] This does not exhaust the list of Canadian complaints on specific practices of United States companies operating in Canada. However, the above survey is intended to be illustrative of only the major areas of Canadian concern.

[16] It is sometimes argued that the inadequacy of these contributions is partly the result of company practices which assign all financial obligations in social welfare to the parent enterprise.

[17] There comes readily to mind the reported parental veto of a Canadian subsidiary's shipment of automobiles to Communist China, on the ground that such trade would violate the foreign-assets-control regulations of the United States Treasury. Address delivered at Arnprior, Ontario, March 28, 1958, by Prime Minister John G. Diefenbaker, The Gazette, Montreal, March 29, 1958, p. 1; also, "Ford China Case: How Ottawa Sees it," The Financial Post, Toronto, March 29, 1958, p. 8. The available evidence suggests that this is not an isolated instance. In any event, it is worth noting that the deep Canadian anxiety seems to spring not so much from the economic impact of such restraints as from the belief that they represent an undue infringement on Canadian sovereignty.

[Since the time of writing, a new facet of this problem has emerged. In November, 1958, the United States Department of Justice filed a civil antitrust suit against

III. SOME TENTATIVE FINDINGS

The swift rise of United States investment in Canada and the intensification of interest in its broad implications have already induced a number of explorations in search of concrete answers to the questions Canadians are now asking about this development. The prime objective has been to put general propositions and hypotheses to the acid test of reason.

Unfortunately, the present state of analysis is not such as to yield positive results over the whole range of issues pervading this field. Nor, in fact, is it at all clear that even the most painstaking inquiry could satisfactorily resolve all of these issues. What is more, where actual findings have been made, they are typically of a tentative nature, subject to revision in the light of further analysis.

Enough thought and research have, nevertheless, been directed at the "investment" problem to warrant outlining their scope and content. This, it is hoped, will provide some insights into the relevant issues and will point the way to the most rewarding lines of future research.

1. Balance and Perspective. The first task is to introduce a sense of balance and perspective into the over-all picture. Canadians would be seriously misguided if, in their preoccupation with "adverse effects," they overlooked the generally harmonious and mutually beneficial climate of currently prevailing Canadian-American relations. It is well to reflect on the words of an eminent scholar in this regard:

The history of debtor-country–creditor-country relations is to many persons largely a history of the evils of modern capitalism, with associations on the one side with "economic imperialism," "colonialism," and "capitalist exploitation," and on the other side with repudiations, confiscations,

two American companies (General Electric Co. and Westinghouse Electric Corp.) and one Netherlands firm (N. V. Phillips' Gloeilampenfabrieken). The principal allegation is that the defendants, through their Canadian subsidiaries, have so operated a patent pool (Canadian Radio Patents Ltd.) as to restrict the flow of United States radio and television equipment into Canada. Eight Canadian companies (including most of the leading firms in Canada's electrical manufacturing industry) are charged as co-conspirators, and relief is being sought in the form of an injunction restraining the defendants' continuance of their allegedly unlawful practices. The general Canadian view is that American antitrust policy should not be applied extra-territorially to cover business practices which are subject to, and not violative of, Canadian law. See "Radio Trust Laid to 3 Big Concerns," The New York *Times*, Nov. 25, 1958, p. 59; also, "U. S. Tries Imposing U. S. Law Here," and "U. S. Holds Big Stick to Our TV, Radio Firms," *The Financial Post*, Toronto, Nov. 29, 1958, pp. 1, 14 respectively.]

and unfair discriminations.   However close this may be to past reality, and it is by no means divorced from historical fact, it has no or only token relationship to the present-day Canadian-American economic realities. The United States of today has no substantial resemblance, whether in the character or the objectives of its government or of its businessmen, to the capital-exporting countries as they are pictured in the histories of imperialism.   Canada as a capital-importing country likewise has no substantial resemblance to the Egypt, the banana republics, or the Balkans of the nineteenth century, in the degree of control over its own political destiny, or in the respect abroad of its legal standards and of its unblemished record of adherence to contractual obligations, or in the extent of its own resources of good government, of capital, of entrepreneurial ability, and of technical skills.   Above all, the relations between the two countries and their peoples, political, economic, geographic, strategic, cultural and psychological, have few if any parallels in the present-day world or in past history in degree of intimacy, harmony, and mutual respect and trust.[18]

No less striking, in the same context, is the observation that

From the search by foreign investors for profit Canada has received a supply of capital, entrepreneurial skills, technological know-how and markets which —for magnitude, quality, and stimulus to domestic growth—has probably never been surpassed anywhere in the world.   There can be no doubt that without this capital inflow Canada's industrial development and living standards could not have approached their present levels.[19]

Clarity of thought also requires a full appreciation of the close interconnections between the "investment" problem and other areas of Canadian-American relations. This is nowhere more true than with respect to commercial policy.   It should be thoroughly understood, for example, that difficulties alleged to derive from United States investment are often rather the product of high American tariff barriers against the importation of Canadian goods. Conversely, what is held to be exclusively a trade problem, namely, Canada's large trade deficits with the United States, turns out to be rooted in Canadian concern over the fact that the deficits are financed substantially by direct-investment inflows into the Canadian economy. It is not easy to avoid blurring these distinctions between trade and investment issues.   But the price of failure is serious misunderstanding, as well

[18] Jacob Viner, "The Gordon Commission Report," *Queen's Quarterly*, LXIV (1957), 312.
[19] Brecher and Reisman, *op. cit.*, pp. 158-159.

as a disjointed approach to the solution of Canadian-American problems.

2. *Company Policies and Practices.* Regarding the policies and practices of United States companies operating in Canada, it should be stated at the outset that the inclination of many Canadians to infer actual from potential nonresident control represents a gross oversimplification of reality. The truth would appear to be that while in many instances such an inference proves to be accurate, in others it does not; that extremes of complete and virtually no actual control are to be found; and that the greatest number of cases are those in which parent and subsidiary share in varying degrees the lines of authority extending over basic policy and operating decisions. Only in part, therefore, can decisions taken at the subsidiary level be deemed to reflect parental conduct.[20]

The evidence relating to company personnel lends additional credence to this conclusion. Personnel and executive development policies, especially in the United States, have been revolutionized during the past generation; one of the effects has been the creation of substantially enlarged opportunities for Canadians to participate in the direction and management of United States-owned companies in Canada. Contrary to popular impression, Canadians typically are now strongly represented on the boards of directors and on the senior executive staffs of such companies.[21] At the same time, it would be wrong to assume that local autonomy is automatically insured by Canadians' filling important posts at the local level. This does provide greater incentives to independent behavior; but it is quite conceivable that Canadian personnel will sometimes act mainly as a conduit for the implementation of company decisions made in the United States. In actual fact, there are more than enough cases of strong parental control to justify serious Canadian interest in the effects of nonresident decisions on the Canadian economy.

The alleged concentration of research functions in the American parent will be recalled in this connection. Here, too, the available

---

[20] The pattern of nonresident control is the product of many factors. Of special significance is the type of business operation in which the enterprise is engaged. More concretely, it is important to distinguish between two classes of Canadian subsidiaries: those which function mainly as raw-material suppliers for their United States parents, and those whose chief purpose is to serve the Canadian market. Corporate policies are often found to differ materially in terms of this distinction.

[21] See especially Empire Trust Company, "American Capital and Canadian Management," *Empire Trust Letter*, Oct., 1958 (New York).

findings are mixed. Extensive fundamental and applied research is carried on in a number of large United States-owned (as well as Canadian-owned) firms producing in Canada's resource-based industries. There are also indications of further development of such facilities in the Canadian operation. Typically, however, it is the parent which, for reasons of cost and efficiency, does the major research; and it is the subsidiary which confines itself to such minor research duties as testing materials and adapting the parent company's products to the Canadian market. Note has already been taken of the prodigious benefits conferred on Canada by this innovation-borrowing process. On the other hand, it seems only reasonable to recognize that continued heavy dependence on outside research may have adverse implications for Canada's future economic growth. "In the rapidly changing fields of product development, the greater gains often accrue to countries with both the initiative and the facilities to take advantage of new opportunities."[22]

The "plant location" issue is much more complex. What is often overlooked is the fact that decisions to locate or expand facilities in the United States are typically based on considerations of economic efficiency and tariff protection. To the extent that Canada loses out, it is likely to be for such reasons rather than because the decisions are taken outside the country. And yet special allowance must be made for those cases in which an American company already has a large investment in United States facilities for manufacturing the particular product whose expansion is being contemplated. Economic analysis supports the view that under such circumstances the most economical decision may well be to use fully the existing equipment before proceeding to expand operations elsewhere; and that given a weak competitive environment, the consequent delay in Canadian development could be of a serious nature. Whether this type of delay has actually materialized and, if so, how far, is a matter for empirical inquiry to establish. The fact is, however, that the available evidence does not provide a satisfactory answer to this question.

By contrast, there is substantial information concerning the export policies of American companies operating in Canada. It would appear that many Canadian subsidiaries are under the strict export control of their United States parents. This control is often exerted by way of outright prohibition or the channeling of the subsidiary's

[22] Brecher and Reisman, *op. cit.*, p. 140.

exports through an export division of the parent company. Admittedly, the export potential of some of these subsidiaries is limited in any event by the existence of tariff barriers and by the fact of superior parental efficiency. It would be useful to know, in more precise terms, how far this is so. But even these are obstacles which an alert and aggressive subsidiary can sometimes overcome. At the very least, it seems clear that for the parent to control a Canadian subsidiary's exports is not only to suppress the latter's initiative and deprive it of opportunities to seek out and develop important new markets, but also to limit its potential for achieving those economies of scale that are so frequently denied to Canadian manufacturing companies hemmed into small markets.

Less is known about purchasing policy. However, there is evidence to suggest that many of the major United States companies operating in Canada deliberately pursue a policy of buying Canadian supplies whenever they are available on competitive terms. On the other hand, there do appear to be cases in which, under parental direction, the subsidiary purchases supplies in the United States which could have been obtained more cheaply in Canada; clearly, these are instances of misallocation which adversely affect both the profitability of the enterprise and the Canadian economy as a whole.

As for the other company practices noted in the preceding section, the available information is sketchy indeed. It simply does not permit a precise judgment as to how far potential dangers are reflected in actual injury to the Canadian economy. Several points are worth making in this connection, however. First, in regard to the rate of resource development, such evidence as has come to light gives strong support to the view that the net effect of United States ownership has been a greatly accelerated, not a retarded, development of Canadian resources. Secondly, past deviations from arm's length pricing in intracompany transactions are to be explained not so much in terms of foreign ownership as of insufficient attention being paid to such transactions by Canada's tax authorities; and recent indications are that this tax defect has been largely remedied. Thirdly, it may well be that only in time of severe economic contraction might Canadian subsidiaries experience greater production cutbacks than if they were Canadian-owned; for only then might the risk of losses become large enough to outweigh the general desire of the American company to protect its Canadian investment. Fourthly, while in some instances the United States parent may discourage its Canadian subsidiary from seeking a reduced American tariff, in others the parent may be an instrument for preserving liberal United States trade measures in the face of protectionist pressures from American producers with no company affiliation in Canada. Fifthly, in the present state of knowledge, the allegation of inadequate company contributions to social welfare is little more than that; the Canadian tendency has been to generalize from a few known cases of limited American participation, despite impressive evidence to the contrary for many other companies.

3. Economic Stability. With regard to the more general economic effects of United States investment, the question arises as to whether it has adverse implications for Canadian stability.[23] A sudden cessation of the capital inflow or a large-scale withdrawal of capital could have serious consequences for Canadian income and employment levels. But it is well to realize that Canada would not be without defenses against such an eventuality. Built into the capital decline would be a drop in Canada's merchandise imports from the United States. In addition, there would be a compensatory depreciation of the Canadian dollar, a drawing-down of Canada's foreign-exchange reserves, and domestic government policy designed to counteract the effects of the capital outflow. All of these factors would provide a significant degree of protection against such a disturbance. But, of greater importance, the chances of this occurring appear quite remote; for much of the United States capital is geared to long-term Canadian development, and only in the unlikely event of a 1929-1933 type of depression, or of precipitate and unfriendly government action against United States interests, might Americans be disposed to reduce their investments on the scale and with the speed assumed.

A second facet of the "stability" argument, as already noted, is that the easy availability of American funds to Canadian subsidiaries of United States companies makes the Canadian economy less amenable to anti-inflationary government policies than would otherwise be the case. This proposition is not as simple as it sounds, because the money supply in Canada is not automatically affected by an inflow of American capital funds; that is, by an exchange of American for Canadian money. Moreover, consideration must be given to the ef-

[23] For a useful discussion of the "stability" and "balance of payments" effects of foreign investment, with special reference to Australia, see H. W. Arndt, "Overseas Borrowing—The New Model," *The Economic Record*, XXXIII (1957), 247-261.

fect of such an inflow on the velocity of spending throughout the economy. The monetary-management implications of large-scale foreign
investment have not been closely explored to date.

4. *"Monopoly," Balance-of-Payments, and Other Questions.* The
"monopoly" argument raises complex problems. It is generally
agreed that "in one way or another the operations of American companies in Canada must exercise an important influence on the quality
and extent of the competition prevailing in the Canadian market."[24]
But to infer monopolistic effects from the fact of large size and concentration is to adopt an oversimplified view of the modern competitive process. It is no less conceivable that in some sectors of the
Canadian economy United States-controlled companies have promoted
competition through such means as new technology, improved product quality, and aggressive merchandising. A determination of actual
results in this sphere must await careful study of the problems involved.

This is also true for the contention that the outflow of nonresident
profits will in the long run constitute an increasing drain on Canada's
financial well-being. One thing seems clear at the outset: there is
no guarantee that such a development will occur. For present purposes, it is sufficient to note that much will depend on the size of the
profit outflow, on the extent and durability of capital inflows, and on
the degree to which such inflows are oriented toward the export
(that is, foreign-exchange-earning) sector of the Canadian economy.

With reference to the "sharing the fruits" argument, it is important for Canadians to acknowledge that "the nonresident investor
who risks his capital and contributes his skills and experience is entitled to reap financial rewards for his efforts. From the Canadian
point of view, this is the necessary price to be paid for rapid economic
progress."[25] At the same time, it is understandable that Canadians
should feel aggrieved over being artificially excluded from equity-
capital participation in a majority of United States enterprises operating in Canada. Such exclusion is made all the more objectionable by
the prospect that in the years to come American capital is likely to
remain dominant in some of the most important and dynamic sectors
of the Canadian economy.[26]

[24] Viner, *op. cit.*, p. 317.   [25] Brecher and Reisman, *op. cit.*, p. 153.
[26] The question often arises as to why so much Canadian capital goes abroad in
the face of a severe shortage of such capital for domestic purposes. Among the

Finally, it should be emphasized that uneasiness about United States control of Canadian industry goes deeper than the question of whether such control has specific adverse effects on the Canadian economy. It is far more a question of national survival, and therefore worth restating in the following terms:

At the root of Canadian concern about foreign investment is undoubtedly a basic, traditional sense of insecurity vis-a-vis our friendly, albeit our much larger and more powerful neighbour, the United States. There is concern that as the position of American capital in the dynamic resource and manufacturing sectors becomes ever more dominant, our economy will inevitably become more and more integrated with that of the United States. Behind this is the fear that continuing integration might lead to economic domination by the United States and eventually to the loss of our political independence.[27]

The honest answer to this "sovereignty" question is that, in the nature of things, there can be no clear-cut answer either way. An objective reading of the history of Canadian-American relations may well suggest that, on balance, these bonds have brought added strength to Canada's position of wealth and power in the world community; that the Canadian entity is now much too solid to succumb to external influence, be it of American or any other origin. But the crux of the matter is that many Canadians remain quite unconvinced by such reasoning. Against this psychological background, it is to be expected that United States investment will persist as a major source of friction in economic relations between the two countries; and that the strongest irritations will stem from those American policies which infringe, however slightly, on the freedom of governmental action in Canada.

---

major factors explaining this paradox are the scarcity in Canada of the huge pools of venture capital necessary for the development of Canadian basic resources, and the inability of Canadians to buy shares in the many domestic corporations wholly owned by United States parents. Then, too, it may well be that substantial amounts of domestic savings are channeled abroad by Canadian insurance companies seeking relatively safe investment outlets. In the light of these considerations, it seems unreasonable to place heavy reliance on the view that Canadians, as individual investors, are by nature more timid than their American counterparts.

[27] Royal Commission on Canada's Economic Prospects, *Final Report*, p. 390. In the same connection, see T. W. Kent, "The American Boom in Canada," *Lloyds Bank Review*, New Series, No. 43 (Jan., 1957), pp. 17-33. And in the broader context of Canadian-American relations, see Michael Barkway, "Canada Rediscovers Its History," *Foreign Affairs*, XXXVI (1958), 409-417; also Bruce Hutchison, "Why Canadians Are Turning Anti-American," *Harper's Magazine*, CCXVI (May, 1958), 46-50.

IV. SUGGESTIONS FOR FURTHER RESEARCH

United States investment has had a mixed impact on the Canadian economy. In very substantial degree, the effects appear to be favorable; to a much lesser extent, adverse; and for the rest, so far indeterminate.[28] Be that as it may, enough has been said to justify the view that this issue merits serious study by all those seeking harmonious economic relations between Canada and the United States. The foregoing analysis will have served a basic purpose if it has indirectly pointed up some of the main areas in which further work on the "investment" problem ought to be undertaken.

1. Company Policies and Practices. One line of inquiry to which early attention might be given centers on the behavior of United States companies operating in Canada. Interest in this area has been consistently strong, and the variety of claims and counterclaims correspondingly great. Recent investigation has made a real contribution toward resolving these issues, especially in the spheres of personnel, company research, and marketing policy. By no means all of the important questions have been answered, however. And where actual results are available, their reliability is often limited by relatively modest coverage of the relevant enterprises.

Two approaches suggest themselves in this connection. One is to survey, through questionnaire and interviews, the policies and practices of a suitably large number of American-controlled companies operating in Canada. Representativeness of the sample would be insured by inclusion of firms of varying size, age, degrees of foreign ownership, and stages of productive activity. On grounds of manageability, the survey would be a selective one; that is, it would not attempt to deal with all facets of company behavior. The criteria of choice should be twofold: the significance of the practice, either in objective terms or in terms of public concern; and the extent to which reasonably precise answers have not already been provided. In this context, initial research effort might be largely devoted to the following areas of decision-making: (1) the location and expansion of industrial plant and facilities in Canada; (2) policies affecting exports and imports of United States-owned subsidiaries doing business in

---

[28] As might be expected, this judgment does not reflect complete unanimity of findings. For an extreme statement to the effect that United States investment raises no problems for Canada, see George Mowbray, " 'Little Canadianism' and American Capital: What Price Economic Nationalism?" *Queen's Quarterly*, LXV (1958), 12-21.

Canada; (3) the production response of these companies to recurrent periods of boom and contraction; and (4) the scope of their participation, financial and otherwise, in Canadian social-welfare activities. This coverage could subsequently undergo such modest expansion as time, cost, and further analysis warrant.

The second approach to company behavior involves concentration on a very small number of United States-controlled enterprises operating in Canada. The purpose here would be, through intensive case study, to shed light on the pattern of control and on the entire range of corporate decisions affecting the Canadian economy. Again, the selection of companies would have due regard for differences in size and age, type of production, and extent of foreign ownership. These studies would, accordingly, be of interest not only for their own sake but also as illustrations of policies and practices over the broad field of American-controlled enterprise.

There would, of course, be some overlapping as between the two "behavior" approaches. For the most part, however, each would complement the other in providing important information about the meaning and effects of United States investment in Canada.

2. *Domestic versus Foreign Financing.* A second high-priority area of study embraces the major obstacles to domestic financing of capital investment in Canada. Of special importance are the investment policies of Canadian insurance companies, comparative tax legislation in Canada and the United States, and the fact that Canadians are denied the opportunity of equity participation in most United States-controlled companies. The lowering of these barriers might go far toward satisfying Canadian aspirations while exerting no prejudicial effect on the over-all position of American capital in Canada. Much is already known about the domestic-financing issue.[29] But there is need for further elaboration—especially upon the problems and prospects of Canadian minority participation in companies now owned wholly in the United States. It is this topic which has most firmly captured Canadian imagination and which probably has the greatest potential for significant results.

3. *Broad Economic Effects.* In the third place, research attention

---

[29] See, for example, Brecher and Reisman, *op. cit.*, chap. vii; J. Grant Glassco, *Certain Aspects of Taxation Relating to Investment in Canada by Non-Residents*, (Royal Commission on Canada's Economic Prospects, Ottawa, 1956); and Empire Trust Company, *Observations on the "Gordon Commission" Recommendations concerning United States Investment in Canada* (New York, 1957).

might usefully be turned to the general economic effects of United States investment on Canada. Among the most interesting questions to be examined are the following: (1) whether the fact of American corporate control has made the Canadian economy more vulnerable to cyclical disturbance; (2) whether United States investment has reduced the scope and degree of effective competition in Canadian industry; (3) whether such investment will in time impose an increasingly heavy burden on Canada's balance of international payments; and (4) whether there are important differences in economic impact as between direct and portfolio investment. Much heat and little light have thus far been generated on these complex issues. The promotion of better understanding here would be a major achievement of economic analysis.

4. Foreign-Investment Policies. Finally, a comparative survey of foreign-investment policies in capital-importing countries, past and present, might well yield worthwhile results. Again, for purposes of manageability, the survey would have to be a selective, not an exhaustive, one. It would, indeed, be sufficient to choose a small group of countries representative of broad geographic areas, different stages of economic development, and varying degrees of national regulation in the foreign-investment field. Special pains should be taken to draw parallels and contrasts between Canada and those countries with which it is most closely associated in terms of culture, economic organization, and political institutions. More generally, Canada's liberal approach to foreign investment could be appraised against the background of national policy and experience throughout the world.

*   *   *   *   *   *   *   *   *   *   *

It will be observed that no research recommendation has been specified for the fundamental "national entity" issue. This omission reflects the judgment that here, as elsewhere, there are limits to the process of reaching precise conclusions from objective analysis. Reference has already been made to the view that, in the unique context of Canadian-American relations, United States investment does not pose a threat to Canadian independence. It has likewise been noted, however, that the grounds for this view cannot be so clear-cut as to convince those who choose to question its validity; and that there are not a few Canadians who have seen fit to make this choice. In the face of such doubts, the overwhelming need would seem to be for general emphasis on the positive aspects of United States investment; and for a sense of appreciation in each country as to the aims and interests of the other.[30]

V. CONCLUDING REFLECTIONS ON PUBLIC POLICY

All this is not to suggest that there can be no scope for public policy in the "United States investment" field; or that such policy must await the filling of the substantial research gaps which still remain. The proper inference is rather that caution and moderation should be the keystone of whatever policy approach may be adopted by Canada's governmental authorities.[31]

1. The Policy Alternatives. Actually, Canadians have expressed widely ranging views on this issue. At one extreme are those who believe that remedial action is not appropriate. This attitude seems to be grounded in one or more of three propositions: the "adverse effects" of United States investment on Canada are either illusory, negligible, or unknown; the future points to a decline in the importance of American investment in Canada; and government intervention would seriously curtail such investment and in consequence greatly retard Canadian economic growth. The line of reasoning here is that public action on this front is quite unnecessary and/or highly undesirable.

At the other extreme are those who would support legislation requiring United States investors to enlarge the area of Canadian participation in American-controlled enterprises operating in Canada. The variety of schemes put forward need not be reviewed here. It is sufficient, in this connection, to note that they have in common the element of compulsion; and that they typically provide for an expanded Canadian share in stock ownership, basic corporate decision-making, and senior technical and management positions. Implicit in

---

[30] "It would be a good thing . . . for both Canadians and non-residents to remember that each is in a position to benefit enormously from the other if they carry out their mutual obligations in a moderate, responsible, and constructive way; and that failure to develop awareness and understanding of the other's position can only lead to common loss." Royal Commission on Canada's Economic Prospects, *Final Report*, p. 400.

[31] There are, to be sure, various avenues of policy open to the United States government. This is especially so in terms of informal suasion bearing on the conduct of American companies operating in Canada. In the nature of the case, however, it seems evident that, to the extent governments are involved, the basic initiative and responsibility must rest with Canada. Consequently, in the discussion which follows, attention will be focused on central questions of Canadian public policy.

this approach is the following rationale: (1) United States investment has serious adverse implications for Canada, both political and
economic; (2) strong measures are needed to cope effectively with
this situation; and (3) in economic terms, Canada would not lose on
balance, and might even gain, from a slowing-down in the pace of
its economic growth.

Between these two approaches is a broad array of views embracing
assorted remedial policies which fall short of coercive regulation.
This intermediate position is most comprehensively exemplified by
the recommendations of the Royal Commission on Canada's Economic Prospects.[32]   On the domestic side, the Commission has suggested that the supply of Canadian capital might be augmented by an
easing of present legislation governing the types of investment which
may be made by life insurance companies and trustees; a case in point
would be the raising of the 15 per cent limitation on investments of
life insurance companies in common stocks.   With the same end in
view, it might also be necessary "to devise new mechanisms for con-
centrating available venture capital and for spreading the risks more
widely."[33]

On the nonresident side, the Commission has recommended three
major lines of action to foreign-owned companies operating in
Canada.[34]

[32] *Final Report,* chap. xviii.   In one sphere, banking and finance, the Commission
is prepared to support the principle of compulsive legislation.   On the ground that
the chartered banks and life insurance companies "form the very core of our financial and business system," the Commission has urged that "appropriate action be
taken to prevent any substantial measure of control of these institutions from coming
into the possession of non-residents." *Ibid.,* p. 397.   In December, 1957, Parliament
enacted legislation providing that a majority of all directors of any insurance company registered in Canada must be Canadian citizens resident in Canada; that the directors of a Canadian life insurance company may refuse to permit transfers of its
shares to persons who are not Canadian citizens resident in Canada, or to corporations
or other organizations established outside Canada or not controlled by Canadian citizens resident in Canada; and that under certain stipulated conditions a Canadian life
insurance company may purchase its own shares for the purpose of converting itself
into a mutual company. *An Act to Amend the Canadian and British Insurance Companies Act (Bill 169),* 23rd Parl., 1st Sess. (1957).

[33] *Final Report,* p. 379.

[34] Canadian policy discussion is typically couched more in terms of foreign investment in general than of United States investment in particular.   This reflects
widespread agreement on the nondesirability of policy measures which discriminate
among nonresident investors.   However, there is little doubt but that the fundamental
Canadian concern relates specifically to American investment; and that foreign-investment policy is characteristically framed with primary reference to United States
holdings in the Canadian economy.

(1) wherever possible, such concerns should employ Canadians in senior management and technical positions, should retain Canadian engineering and other professional and service personnel, and should do their purchasing of supplies, materials and equipment in this country;

(2) they should publish their financial statements and make full disclosure of the results of their Canadian operations;

(3) they should include on their boards of directors a number of independent Canadians and they should sell an appreciable interest [20 per cent to 25 per cent] in their equity stock to Canadians.[35]

As far as the Commission is concerned, such conduct is a matter of enlightened self-interest for the enterprises involved. However, some doubt is expressed as to whether suasion alone would be sufficient to achieve the objective of increased corporate control by Canadians. It is, accordingly, suggested that the increased depreciation allowances recommended for Canadian industry be made conditional, in their application to nonresident firms, upon such firms' complying with the Commission's request on directorates and equity stock; that the same condition should attach to foreign-company enjoyment

[35] *Final Report*, p. 393. More generally, some Canadians have suggested construction of a model "code of behavior" for the guidance of foreign-owned companies doing business in Canada. See, for example, G. Huson, "How A Foreign Subsidiary Can Win Friends in Canada," *The Business Quarterly*, XXIII (1958), 34-36.

In certain instances, recommendations on company behavior might be more directly applicable to the home government of the parent firm. Such would be the case, for example, where United States law prohibited parent companies from allowing their Canadian (and other) subsidiaries to engage in practices considered legal by the Canadian government authorities. Indeed, some action along these lines has already been taken: "The Canadian and United States governments have given consideration to situations where the export policies and laws of the two countries may not be in complete harmony. It has been agreed that in these cases there will be full consultation between the two governments with a view to finding through appropriate procedures satisfactory solutions to concrete problems as they arise." Joint Communique issued in Ottawa by President Eisenhower and Prime Minister Diefenbaker, July 9, 1958, as quoted in *The Gazette*, Montreal, July 10, 1958, p. 1. Just what operational meaning this agreement will have is not clear. On the whole, official Canadian interpretations have been somewhat more sympathetic to the Canadian viewpoint than have been the explanatory statements issued by United States authorities.

[Since the time of writing, the Canadian and United States governments have discussed the problem of extra-territorial application of American antitrust law. (See footnote 17 above.) In January, 1959, Canada's Minister of Justice and the Attorney-General of the United States announced agreement on prior consultation in cases of this kind which might arise in the future. Again, only time can give content to such an approach. Meanwhile, still unresolved is the issue of whether the United States government will proceed with the antitrust court action already launched in the radio-television industry. See "U. S. Will 'Consult' in Canadian Casses," *The Gazette*, Montreal, Jan. 30, 1959, p. 1.]

of certain tax concessions proposed for Canada's oil and gas industries; and that only complying nonresident firms should benefit from the special 5 per cent withholding tax on dividend income (other foreign companies to pay the general nonresident rate of 15 per cent).[36]

2. *Major Criteria for Choice.* On reflection, it will be recognized that Canadian policy-makers could, with relative ease, devise a wide variety of specific remedies consistent with the intermediate approach. Much more difficult is the question as to how far, if at all, the technique of informal suasion should be supplemented by legislative action directly affecting foreign investment.[37] Other things being equal, there is a strong likelihood that the latter technique will achieve more tangible results. But other things may not be equal; to set a precedent of legislation, however mild, which discriminates against nonresidents with investment in Canada might be to exert a dragging effect on Canadian economic growth. These are the conflicting considerations to be weighed in any rational decision on the content of noncompulsory policy in the "United States investment" field.[38]

Indeed, the same factors are also pertinent to the more basic choice between the intermediate approach as a whole and that of formally requiring increased Canadian participation in the foreign-investment sector of the Canadian economy. Here, however, the countervailing forces are more pronounced. On the one hand, it is clear that compulsory legislation is better designed to enlarge the resident-investment share. On the other hand, it is equally clear that the compulsory approach is more likely to retard Canada's

[36] No tax restrictions would be imposed on foreign financing of fixed-interest obligations. Indeed, the Commission has urged that non-residents be encouraged to channel a larger share of their Canadian investments into mortgages and government and corporate bonds. *Final Report,* pp. 392, 398.

[37] The principle of direct government encouragement, through legislation or otherwise, of capital accumulation and investment by Canadians is not really in issue here. It would presumably find general acceptance among those who favor some measure of public intervention in the area of capital financing.

[38] To an appreciable extent, informal suasion is already in effect as an instrument of Canadian government policy. The case of conflict between United States and Canadian laws on foreign trade was cited above (footnote 35). More generally, see, for example, the Address delivered to the Canadian Club of Chicago, Oct. 15, 1956, by Mr. C. D. Howe, then Minister of Trade and Commerce, *External Affairs,* VIII (1956), 352-354; Address at Dartmouth College, Hanover, N. H., Sept. 7, 1957, by Prime Minister Diefenbaker, *External Affairs,* IX (1957), 274-276; and Address delivered to the Investment Bankers Association of America, Hollywood Beach, Fla., Dec. 2, 1957, by Mr. Donald M. Fleming, Minister of Finance, *The Gazette,* Montreal, Dec. 3, 1957, p. 19.

economic development by reducing the country's attractiveness as an outlet for nonresident investment funds. Nor does it suffice to argue that a slower pace of growth would not be detrimental to Canadian economic welfare. Quite apart from the merits of this contention— and they are open to serious question—it is probable that most Canadians would be unwilling to support policies which entailed a substantial slowing-down of national economic development.[39] If this judgment is sound, it follows that the noncompulsory investment approach has the more solid claim to governmental adoption.

But there is a further basic choice to be made—between this intermediate approach and a policy of nonintervention in the foreign-investment sphere. The latter alternative is not without strength. For one thing, it is the only approach entirely free of potential restraint on Canadian economic growth. Secondly, where adverse economic effects of United States investment can be identified, they would appear to be minor by comparison with its enormous economic benefits. Thirdly, in considerable degree the direction and intensity of the American impact have not thus far been revealed by economic analysis. There is, in the fourth place, good reason to believe that over the next quarter century, given present policies, foreign ownership and control will decline relative to the Canadian economy as a whole.

At the same time, the factors militating against complete laissez-faire are most impressive. Even in the face of wide research gaps, the available evidence does establish the fact of some adverse economic influence on Canada stemming from United States investment; the judgment that it is relatively minor does not make its amelioration or removal a matter of indifference to Canadian public policy. Nor does the anticipated relative decline in over-all foreign ownership and control tell, by any means, the whole story of future prospects; of special significance is the point that for certain sectors of the Canadian economy—and more particularly for those industries in which foreign investment is now dominant—it seems reasonable to expect a continued rise in the nonresident share over the years to come. But perhaps the crucial consideration is the deep-rooted Cana-

[39] There is, of course, no way of gauging accurately Canadian public opinion on the "growth" issue. Nor is there any intention of minimizing the force of national concern over the "politics" of United States investment in Canada. Nevertheless, it does seem fair to suggest that current Canadian thinking, to the extent it has been articulated, would in general regard substantially curtailed economic growth as too high a price to pay for reduced American ownership and control of Canadian industry.

dian concern over the social and political implications of large and increasing United States investment in the Canadian economy. It has already been suggested that this concern may well be without objective foundation in the modern context of Canadian development and Canada-United States relations. This does not go to the heart of the matter, however. The basic truth is that in the minds of many Canadians the "sovereignty" issue poses a very real and vital problem; and that moderate remedial action could contribute to its solution without appreciably weakening the external stimulus to Canadian economic growth.

* * * * * * * * * * *

It remains only to add the conviction that, in the last analysis, the main burden of constructive effort in the "United States investment" sphere must be borne not by specific measures of public policy but rather by mutual respect and understanding. For Canadians, this means, in essence, preventing an exaggerated sense of national pride from distorting the real investment picture; and realizing that undue emphasis on matters of controversy obscures the overwhelmingly important contribution made by United States capital to Canadian economic development. For Americans, the prime task would appear to be that of overcoming a traditional deficiency of interest in matters of Canadian concern; and, more concretely, giving full recognition to the fact that American capital is not viewed in Canada as an entirely unmixed blessing, especially in so far as it fails to provide for a high degree of local autonomy in the operations of United States companies doing business in Canada.

There is, indeed, a broader frame of reference for these concluding comments:

Canadian and United States interdependence demands a new category of relationship . . . . The concept to be realized in the best interests of both countries is that of free and powerful nations of different background and capabilities, united through a basic agreement on values and aspirations, and voluntarily joined in enterprises, domestic and foreign, calculated to strengthen the chances for a world reflecting their common values. This is the challenge for Canadian-United States relations.[40]

[40] *Hays-Coffin Report*, p. 15. See also *Second Hays-Coffin Report* (Washington, 1958), which appeared after the time of writing; and Jacob Viner, *Canada and Its Giant Neighbour* (Ottawa, 1958).

7

The Influence of American Labor Organizations and Policies on Canadian Labor

Eugene Forsey

I

The influence of American labor organizations and policies on Canadian labor, like the influence of American everything else on Canadian everything else, is enormous, and mainly for the same reasons. How could it be otherwise? Canada and the United States are closer together, physically, economically, socially, culturally, than any other two large countries in the world. The United States is immeasurably the bigger and richer of the two. Canada is heavily dependent on the United States for markets, for supplies of things we cannot grow or make ourselves, for capital, and for technology. We read American books and magazines, we listen to American radio, we watch American television, we buy American branded goods. Americans control some of our most important industries. Canada is emphatically an American nation, in every sense of the word "American," and Canadian labor can no more escape from that fact than Canadian government, Canadian business, Canadian art, music, literature, Canadian science, Canadian religion, Canadian sport, Canadian anything.

But Canada is not *just* an American nation, a satellite, a fiftieth state, a thirteenth federal reserve district, a pale carbon copy of the United States. It is not only an American nation, it is a British American nation. We are independent, but we belong to the British Commonwealth. The very name of our written Constitution, "the British North America Act," proclaims the fact, and each successive amendment, each a "British North America Act," proclaims it afresh. Our working Constitution is a British, parliamentary Constitution, "similar in principle," as the Act of 1867 says, "to the Constitution of the United Kingdom." That is the rock on which our political institutions are built.

Canada is also a French American nation. Nearly a third of our people speak French. Their whole Civil Law is French. They have a French Church, which, in Quebec, is an established church, with the legal right to collect the tithe from its members, and to control all the schools except the dissentient schools of the "Queen's Protestant subjects." French is one of the two official languages of the Parliament of Canada and of the Dominion courts, and, of the legislature and courts of Quebec. Our national radio and television system has French networks. We have big French universities, a large French press, a French theater, a flourishing French culture.

Canada is the only nation on this continent which has deliberately chosen not to break with its past, both British and French. For Canadians the most important thing about the American Revolution is that we refused to have anything to do with it. We refused then, and again in 1812, to be "liberated." We deliberately chose to keep our roots, and draw nourishment from them. We have repeatedly reaffirmed that decision, notably at Confederation, when, as Sir John A. Macdonald said at the time, we could perfectly well have severed the tie which bound us to Great Britain.

Canada is also the only nation on this continent which has deliberately chosen to preserve not one heritage but two. The United States deliberately chose to make itself a nation of one language and one culture. Canada deliberately chose not to.

Canada is also a Canadian nation. It is American, it is British, it is French. But it is not just a mixture of the three. There are things about it which are neither American, nor British, nor French, but simply Canadian; things we have developed ourselves; ways of doing things—things political, things economic, things social, things artistic, things literary, things religious—which are neither American, nor British, nor French. Even our two languages are to some extent our own; our English is certainly not the same as English English or Scots English or American English; and our French is not the same as French French or Swiss French or Belgian French. I do not say that our English is worse than English or Scots or American English, or our French worse than French or Swiss or Belgian French. But they are not identical. They have their own distinctive character.

II

That is the framework within which this subject has to be considered if we want to arrive at conclusions which will mean anything. Canadian labor has always been powerfully influenced by American labor organizations and policies, and always will be, as far ahead as anyone can see. It would have been powerfully influenced even if there had been no organic connection between the Canadian and American movements. It would still be powerfully influenced even if that connection should come to an end, a development of which there seems to be not the slightest possibility. But American influence has never had things all its own way. It has always had to contend against the British tradition,[1] the French-Canadian tradition, and Canadian nationalism generally. It probably always will. British influence may weaken, the French-Canadian tradition may be largely absorbed in the wider Canadian nationalism; but Canadian nationalism, in Canadian unions as in other Canadian institutions, will wax rather than wane.

In fact, of course, the influence of American labor organizations and policies on Canadian labor has exercised itself mainly through the fact that most Canadian organized workers belong to "international" unions: unions whose headquarters, and most of whose membership, are in the United States. At the moment, about 1,454,000 of Canada's 4,578,000 wage and salary earners are organized. About 690,000 of the 4,578,000 are "managerial and professional." So about 37 per cent of the theoretically organizable workers are organized. Of the 1,454,000 organized workers, 73 per cent, are in international unions.[2] As far back as official figures go, which is nearly half a century, international unions have had anywhere from 51 per cent to 90 per cent of our total union membership. The percentage fluctuated downward from 90 per cent in 1911 to 51 per cent in

[1] The first "international" unions in Canada were British. The Amalgamated Society of Engineers established its first local in Canada in 1850, followed by three more in 1851. The Amalgamated Society of Carpenters and Joiners in 1860 became the first permanent union in the building trades. The A.S.E. was absorbed into the International Association of Machinists in 1920, and the A.S.C.J. into the United Brotherhood of Carpenters and Joiners in 1914, though some branches seceded in 1922 and resumed their status as locals of the British organization till 1925, when the latter finally withdrew from Canada.

[2] Department of Labour, *Labour Organization in Canada*, 1958 (Ottawa, 1958), p. 11; *The Labour Force*, 1958; and mimeographed sheet of "persons with jobs" by industry (DBS).

1935, then rose unevenly to approximately 70 per cent, and has fluctuated around that figure for the past ten years.[3] (See Appendix Table 20.)

Even this does not tell the whole story. The five biggest unions, with a total Canadian membership of almost 310,000, are all international. Seventeen of the biggest twenty-one are international, and for these twenty-one the membership of the internationals outnumbers that of the nationals by over five and a half to one. About three-quarters of all unions in Canada with a membership of over 10,000 are international. In the forty leading manufacturing industries, international unions have about 85 per cent of the total membership. Except for the fishing industry on both coasts, the Quebec asbestos and aluminum industries, and part of the Quebec pulp and paper industry, almost all the organized workers in the big export industries belong to international unions. There are only four national unions with over 20,000 members, against 16 international. Except for the National Catholic unions in Quebec, national unions "play a relatively minor role."[4]

International unions are, beyond question, "the dominant force in Canadian organized labour";[5] and the American membership is the dominant force in every international union. There are only 23 of the whole 111 operating in Canada in which the Canadian membership is more than 10 per cent of the total, one where it is over 40 per cent, two where it is over 25 per cent, and six where it is over 20 per cent.[6] (See Appendix Table 22.)

There is nothing like this anywhere else in the world, and it has been a perennial subject of uneasiness, real or feigned, among Canadian employers,[7] some groups of Canadian workers, and considerable

[3] Brecher and Reisman, *Canada-United States Economic Relations*, p. 205, Table 32.

[4] *Labour Organization in Canada*, 1958, pp. 13-17; Brecher and Reisman, *op. cit.*, pp. 202-203.

[5] *Ibid.*, p. 202.

[6] *Labour Organization in Canada*, 1957, pp. 15-20; *Directory of National and International Unions in the United States*, 1957, Bulletin No. 1222, U. S. Department of Labor, pp. 30-46.

[7] In the spring of 1958, there was a sudden spate of violent attacks on international unionism by Canadian employers and newspapers. This may have been partly a matter of people who disliked unions *per se* seizing on the United States Senate Committee's disclosures of malpractices in the American sections of certain international unions as a convenient stick with which to beat the Canadian sections of all international unions. It may also have been partly a reaction to sharp criticism of

sections of the general public. Obviously, they have argued, most of the Canadian trade union movement is just a colony of the American. In the face of these figures, how can it be anything else? And a "colonial" union movement, dominated from below the border, is not only inconsistent with Canadian sovereignty but dangerous to Canadian interests.

III

The figures are impressive. They look decisive. But they are not. The reality is altogether different.

In the first place, the main Canadian central labor organization, the Canadian Labour Congress (CLC), is, by its constitution, a completely autonomous body. It has friendly, fraternal, relations with the AFL-CIO, but it is not chartered by the AFL-CIO, does not pay dues to the AFL-CIO, is not subsidized by the AFL-CIO. The AFL-CIO, in fact, "hath no jurisdiction in this realm of Canada," except for certain trade departments; and the CLC Constitution, Article XI, provides for the supersession of these "when deemed desirable and feasible."[8]

Nor does the CLC take its policies from the AFL-CIO. In legislative matters, which are one of its main concerns, it cannot, because so

---

a Canadian Royal Commission report by the American president of an international union. The Royal Commission had reported that firemen were no longer needed on diesel locomotives in freight and yard service on the Canadian Pacific Railway. Mr. H. E. Gilbert, President of the Brotherhood of Locomotive Firemen and Enginemen, issued from Cleveland, Ohio, a denunciation of the Commission as "inept or incompetent." This was naturally resented. Few, if any, of those who, in turn, denounced Mr. Gilbert for interfering in a purely Canadian dispute seem to have realized that the disappearance of firemen from freight and yard diesels on the C.P.R. can scarcely fail to threaten their continued use on similar jobs with American railways. The report must inevitably have repercussions of the most serious kind for the whole American membership of the Firemen. Anyhow, Mr. Percy M. Fox, Mr. Norris R. Crump, the Alberta Associated Chambers of Commerce, the Saskatchewan Employers' Association, and a chorus of newspapers, large and small, let fly with a series of attacks about international unions being run by "labour bosses," "crooks and grafters," people with "an alien approach to Canadian needs"; about Canada's economic integrity being "placed in jeopardy and at the whim and to serve the special interests of some union leaders in the United States"; etc., etc. See, for example: Montreal *Gazette,* May 1 and 29, 1958; Edmonton *Journal,* June, 12, 1958; Quebec *Le Soleil,* May 30, 1958; Toronto *Globe and Mail,* May 22, 1958; Moose Jaw *Times-Herald,* May 22, 1958; Regina *Leader-Post,* May 14, 1958.

[8] Resolutions on this subject were presented but not passed at the 1958 convention. It should be noted that the CLC handles its own jurisdictional problems. So did the Canadian Congress of Labour (CCL). The Trades and Labor Congress (TLC) followed the decisions of the AFL.

much of the most important legislation is so different from the American. For example, labor relations in Canada are almost wholly under provincial jurisdiction, with ten different acts, none of them much like any American act. Unemployment insurance in Canada is a single national scheme, with the employees paying 41⅔ per cent of the cost and the national government 16⅔ per cent plus administration. Old age security is a system of flat rate benefits, financed, for all practical purposes, out of general taxation. Family allowances, of course, simply do not exist in the United States. Workmen's compensation in Canada is run by provincial government boards, and financed wholly by assessments on employers. The Canadian Housing Act differs widely from its American counterpart. The CLC and its provincial Federations simply cannot just copy AFL-CIO legislative demands, because they would be in most cases completely irrelevant, pointless, "words and breath."

On foreign affairs, the CLC could follow the AFL-CIO, but it doesn't, notably in the matter of recognition of Communist China, which it has repeatedly pressed upon the government. On political action, following the AFL-CIO policy would be difficult, first because under our parliamentary responsible government, Members of Parliament do not have individual "records"

> ("When in that House, M.P.'s. divide,
> If they've a brain and cerebellum, too,
> They've got to leave that brain outside,
> And vote just as their leaders tell 'em to");

and second, because the chances of labor getting into one of the two old parties and exerting any real influence in it are microscopic. But even if the CLC could follow the AFL-CIO political action policy, it is not doing so. Independent labor political action has been a recurrent theme all through the history of the Canadian trade union movement (partly, no doubt, because of the British example, transmitted by British immigrants), and the CLC appears now to be in process of launching a third party, something the AFL-CIO is not even thinking about.

Canadian labor had to struggle for the autonomy it now enjoys. The AFL persisted, right down to 1955, in chartering local unions in Canada. It also made repeated attempts to deny to its Canadian counterpart, the Trades and Labor Congress of Canada, the right to charter local Trades and Labor Councils, and it took the TLC thirty-five years (1910-1945) to win out. The AFL also virtually forced the TLC to expel the Canadian branches of CIO unions. The TLC balked in 1936, 1937 and 1938. But in 1939 it gave in. And beyond question, I think, Canadian labor would have achieved reunion years before it did had it not been for the situation in the United States.

It may be asked, if the AFL could break labor unity in Canada in 1939, and keep it broken till 1956, why can't the AFL-CIO do the same thing now? The answer, I think, is twofold.

First, the CLC is not, constitutionally, in the same position as the TLC was. The TLC constitution forbade the affiliation of any union whose jurisdiction conflicted with that of any union already affiliated. In effect, it could not admit, or keep, unions "dual" to AFL unions. Once the Committee for Industrial Organization, in 1938, became the Congress of Industrial Organizations, thus setting the seal upon the fact that it was "dual" to the AFL, the TLC found itself in a box. It really had to choose between losing the CIO unions, with a membership of perhaps 50,000 at most, or the AFL unions, with a membership of well over 100,000. And as long as the AFL unions felt that way, the TLC was in the same box. Not until the AFL was prepared to make honest women of the CIO unions could the TLC take any decisive steps toward unity in Canada.[9] But the CLC constitution contains no such clause as that TLC clause whose mortal taste brought, if not death, at least fifteen years of disunity, into the Canadian labor movement, and much of our woe.

The second reason why 1939 could not be repeated is the growth of Canadian nationalism in Canadian unions. Canadian union members now just would not stand for anything of the sort. Even before the merger of the TLC and the CCL, in 1956, the CCL had refused to take in at least two CIO unions, had thrown out another some time before the CIO did, and had kept two others which the CIO had expelled. (Both these last are in the CLC, though still outside the AFL-CIO.) More significant, the TLC itself, in 1946, refused to throw out the Machinists at the behest of the AFL, and it kept the International Longshoremen's Association when the AFL expelled it. (The Longshoremen are in the CLC, though outside the AFL-

[9] See Eugene Forsey, "The Movement Towards Labour Unity in Canada: History and Implications," *Canadian Journal of Economics and Political Science*, XXIV (1958), 70-83, especially pp. 77-78.

CIO.) Most significant of all are certain events of the last year in the two central organizations. The AFL-CIO, at its last convention, suspended several unions. All of them are still affiliated with the CLC. If the CLC were the subservient, colonial appendage of the AFL-CIO that it is sometimes made out to be, it would have lost no time in following the example of its American counterpart. Instead, at the April, 1958, CLC Convention, there was not so much as a suggestion of any such action. On the contrary, the CLC threw out two unions, the Operating Engineers and the Technical Engineers, which are still in the bosom of the AFL-CIO.

IV

True enough, say the critics of international unionism; but the real power in Canadian trade unionism lies not with the central organization but with the constituent unions. They have the money. They have the organizers. They do the bargaining. They decide the economic policies, and (within the limits set by the Canadian Constitution, laws, and institutions) the political policies too, of Canadian unionism. The real question is, What happens inside each individual international union? How much "autonomy" do the Canadian locals enjoy?

The answer is that for all practical purposes, and with rare exceptions, the autonomy is complete.

A good many Canadians outside the labor movement find this very hard, even impossible, to believe. They are convinced that the American leaders, or the American membership, or both, are bound to ride roughshod over the Canadian members, misleading, oppressing, plundering.

There are several reasons why this is not true.

One is that the American leaders and members in most cases don't know enough about Canada to do an effective job of misleading, oppressing, and plundering even if they wanted to. Another is that they don't care enough; after all, in most cases the Canadian membership is pretty small beer. Still a third is that the plunder isn't big enough to make the effort worth while.

Even the best informed American labor research people usually know relatively little about Canada, Canadian conditions, Canadian laws, Canadian ways of doing things; they are generally just too busy to have time to mug it up. The officers of their unions, being even busier, probably know even less and have certainly even less time to learn. They must perforce leave most of the leadership and policy-making and administration in Canada to Canadians.

As for caring: the late J. L. Cohen, a very prominent Canadian labor lawyer, used to tell a story about the early days of the CIO in Canada. All over industrial Ontario, little local unions were spring-ing up, calling themselves CIO, though the CIO had never heard of them. Mr. Cohen and Mr. C. H. Millard, one of the early Cana-dian CIO leaders, decided to go down to CIO headquarters to ask for help for these struggling Canadian locals. They went. They saw the CIO chief organizer. He listened to their fervent appeal. He was most sympathetic. He assured them the CIO wanted to help. But it couldn't just then, because it had first to organize the continen-tal United States, then Alaska. Then it would go on to Canada. This was at a time when, according to many respectable Canadians, the CIO leaders were sitting up nights seeking how they might devour Canadian workers! I do not suggest that the attitude of that par-ticular early CIO organizer is typical. But I think it is a good deal nearer the truth than the notion that the chief desire of American union leaders is to rope in Canadian members and lead them round by the nose.

The United Mine Workers is often considered a rather highly centralized union. It is headed by a gentleman who is not usually regarded as lacking in force of character, and is, I understand an ar-dent devotee of "free enterprise." The United Mine Workers has two Canadian districts. One of them, in 1938, affiliated, en bloc, with the Co-operative Commonwealth Federation, the Canadian equivalent of the British Labour party. Did international head-quarters order District 26 to disaffiliate from the CCF? Not a bit of it. The District is still an autonomous district of the UMW and still affiliated with the CCF. Furthermore, when the UMW was play-ing in-again-out-again-off-again-on-again in the United States, into the CIO, out of it, into the AFL, out of it, the Canadian districts through-out stayed affiliated with the CCL, the Canadian counterpart of the CIO; indeed, the chief executive officer of the CCL was a UMW man. Against this must be set the fact that the UMW in Canada has stayed out of the CLC, and I think there is little doubt that the influence of international headquarters played a part in this, perhaps a decisive part. But in the main, even in this highly centralized union, Canadian autonomy has been respected.

What about the plunder? One of the commonest charges in Canada against international unions is that they take large sums of money out of Canadian workers' pockets, and out of the country, in the form of union dues and assessments. This is like the celebrated report of Mark Twain's death, only more so.

In the first place, the dues are not nearly so big as many people suppose. Brecher and Reisman give figures for 70 of the largest international unions in Canada. Most of them run about $2.00 to $3.50 per month.[10]

Second, only part of the dues ("variously estimated at one-third to one-half," say Brecher and Reisman[11]) goes to international headquarters.

Third, most of this is deposited in Canadian banks and used to pay for national and district Canadian offices, dues to the CLC, organization, research, education, and strike pay.[12]

Fourth, very large payments come into Canada from international unions, notably for strike pay. It is not easy to get precise figures on this, chiefly because the published accounts of international unions do not segregate their Canadian operations. But there are occasional indications of what probably is happening and has happened ever since international unions entered Canada about a hundred years ago. In 1926, for example, I made a calculation for District 26 of the United Mine Workers, which first came into Nova Scotia in 1908. Adding up regular dues and assessments going out, and strike pay coming in, it seemed clear that at least $1,000,000 more must have come in from the United States than went out to it. Of course this was a particularly turbulent period, with several prolonged strikes. But it must have taken a long period of calm for the regular dues of the 12,000 or so Nova Scotia members to make up to the international union for what it had sent in. In the northern Ontario gold mine strike of a few years ago, it was widely reported in union circles that the Steel Workers had spent $2,000,000 on strike pay. It would take 75,000 Canadian Steel Workers almost eighteen months to pay that sum in dues to the international union. In 1955 the United Automobile Workers, according to its Canadian Director, paid out $2,160,-

---

[10] *Op. cit.*, Appendix D, pp. 304-315.   [11] *Ibid.*, p. 213.
[12] *Ibid.*

ooo in strike pay while the Canadian membership, in the first eleven months, paid only $1,169,000 into the union's special strike fund (regular per capita dues to the international union on 60,000 members would have been about $900,000 for the whole year). Perhaps figures like these help to explain why international unions' accounts do not segregate their Canadian operations; the American membership might begin to grumble that these Canadians cost too much!

It may be well to add that I know of no cases where American union leaders have "stolen" Canadian unions. For one thing, the pickings are too small to be attractive; a corrupt American union leader can easily find much bigger ones at home. For another, our criminal law is national, so that the thief cannot play hop, skip, and jump from province to province. For a third, all our judges are appointed by the national government, for life or till they are seventy-five, so that there is no chance of influencing them through local political machines. The thief has little to gain, and is almost certain to be caught, and promptly and severely punished.

Canadian locals and Canadian districts of international unions are almost invariably led and staffed by Canadians. In the few cases where the vice-president or director or manager in charge of Canadian affairs is, or has been, an American citizen, he has at times identified himself so completely with the Canadian membership and its interests that he has become a more perfervid Canadian nationalist than his Canadian colleagues! On occasion, Canadian locals or districts have been put under "administration" or trusteeship by the international union, or Canadian staff members have been dismissed when an international convention has elected a new slate of officers. But this applies equally to American locals and districts and American staff. There is not, as far as I know, the slightest evidence that Canadians have been proceeded against as Canadians, or treated one whit differently from Americans. The administrators or trustees have usually, if not always, been Canadians, and displaced Canadian officials have been replaced by Canadians.

There is, as a rule, only one real limitation on the autonomy of Canadian locals or districts of international unions: in most cases, they cannot go on strike without the approval of international headquarters. But this also applies equally to American locals and districts. It is not a limitation on Canadian autonomy but simply on local union or district autonomy. It is imposed for the simple and practical reason that, as the international union must generally foot the bill for strike pay, it dare not give its locals or districts, American or Canadian, a blank check.

There is a fairly widespread belief in Canada that the headquarters of any international union can order the Canadian membership to go on strike. For this notion there appears to be no warrant whatever. The eminently respectable, employer-sponsored National Industrial Conference Board, a few years ago, analyzed no less than 194 national and international American union constitutions, covering 17,500,000 members, or about 98 per cent of the whole union movement in the United States. If there were any international unions which slipped through its net, they must have been small indeed, and their Canadian membership could probably have been put into a few taxis or a single bus. What did the analysis show?

One hundred and three constitutions, covering 60.5 per cent of the membership, vested final authority to approve locally authorized strikes in the international union. Two constitutions, covering 3.5 per cent of the membership, required international approval of important strikes but allowed purely local strikes if the local bore the whole cost. Twenty-three constitutions, covering 16.2 per cent of the membership, allowed the locals to strike without international approval, but stipulated that in such cases there would be no money forthcoming from the international treasury. Nine constitutions, covering 3.9 per cent of the membership, vested sole authority to authorize strikes in the international union. Ten constitutions, covering 4.1 per cent of the membership, allowed locals to strike without any international union approval. Thirteen constitutions, covering 3.4 per cent of the membership, prohibited strikes altogether. Twenty-nine constitutions, covering 7.8 per cent of the membership, had no provisions at all on strike authorization.[13] The NICB analysis does not record a single case where there was special provision for Canadian strikes, nor a single case where an international union was empowered to "order" a strike.

That, however, is something of a digression from the main question, how far the Canadian sections of international unions are really autonomous. Let us get back to it.

[13] National Industrial Conference Board, Inc., *Handbook on Union Government Structure and Procedures* (New York, 1955), p. 42.

V

Granted, say the critics (though I am not sure how many of them would in fact be willing to grant it), that most Canadian sections of international unions are formally led and their affairs managed by Canadians. Granted that most of the larger international unions have Canadian vice-presidents or executive board members, sometimes two or three,[14] and that at least some of these wield considerable influence at international headquarters. Granted that the Canadian membership may sometimes be numerous enough, and well enough organized, to hold the balance of power at international conventions. Granted that international headquarters may very rarely actually order the Canadian sections to adopt American policies, and cannot order them to strike. Doesn't the real power still lie with international headquarters? The American leaders are usually powerful personalities. They usually have a record of conspicuous successes in their own country. Their own, and their policies', prestige is very great. Surely they can exercise enormous influence without issuing a single order, without so much as a hint of coercion, without even using the power of the purse and keeping the Canadian sections on short commons? In effect, if not in form, can't the American majority force the Canadian minority to adopt wage and other policies which are not suited to Canadian conditions, and might gravely injure the Canadian economy and Canadian workers?

Theoretically, I suppose, the answer is "Yes." Practically, the answer is "It could, but it hasn't and it won't." Stephen Leacock, in his lectures on the British Constitution, when I was an undergraduate at McGill, used to say: "Foreigners often ask, 'What would happen if the King used all his legal powers?' The answer is, 'He won't.' 'What would happen if the House of Lords used all its legal powers?' The answer is, 'It won't.'" It is the same with the international trade union movement on this continent.

Canadian employers sometimes assert that Canadian workers adopt wage and other policies which are not suited to Canadian conditions. They sometimes go on to assert that this is because most Canadian workers belong to international unions. The first asser-

[14] Brecher and Reisman, *op. cit.*, p. 210, say they found Canadian members on the boards of two-thirds of 93 unions they examined. Their Appendix D, pp. 304-315, giving details for 70, shows 50 with one or more Canadians on their boards. The number is certainly higher now.

tion, true or false, does not concern us here. The second does. The theory seems to be that if the Ford workers in Windsor, Ontario, for example, had not belonged to an international union, the UAW, it would never have occurred to them to ask for the guaranteed annual wage. If they had looked across the river and seen what the American employees of the American Ford Company were asking for, and in part getting, they would just have said, "Well, well! Most interesting!" The idea that Canadian workers have to eat, and pay rent, and clothe themselves all the year round, just as much as American workers, would never have crossed their minds. Nobody would have thought of asking, "If it's good for the man on the Ford assembly line in Detroit, why not for the man on the Ford assembly line in Windsor?"

Of course the international union's policy for its American members influenced its Canadian members. But, short of erecting a Chinese Wall or an Iron Curtain between Canada and the United States, there is just no way of preventing Canadian workers from finding out what American workers are doing; and when they find out, they are very likely to think that what is good for American workers is good for Canadian also, and ask for it. If every single union in Canada were simon-pure Canadian, if not a single unionist in Canada had ever so much as laid eyes on an American union member, the result would be precisely what it is now, or so nearly the same that it would need an electron microscope to see the difference.

In this connection Brecher and Reisman say:

In general it is the Canadian local, not international headquarters, which determines the scope and content of union requests with respect to wages, hours of work, fringe benefits and the other objectives sought through collective bargaining. Moreover, international headquarters rarely exercises its power of approval in such a way as to require changes in the contracts negotiated by the Canadian locals.

.   .   .   .

Trade union experience across the border, often in negotiations with the same corporation, is quite naturally drawn upon by Canadian locals; so too is the technical advice of common personnel always available at headquarters. Furthermore headquarters officials sometimes participate directly in Canadian negotiations; but to the extent they do, this is normally at the invitation of the Canadian local, in an advisory and technical capacity, within the framework of requests established by the local. . . .[15]

They also point out, significantly, that "purely Canadian unions . . . display behaviour patterns quite similar to those in the United States."[16] But, being usually bigger and richer, international unions are perhaps usually more successful in getting what they go after. "There's the rub," perhaps, from the employers' point of view. The fault may not be so much their Americanness as their success.

It is sometimes asserted that the Canadian sections of international unions are trying to get the same wages here as in the United States, in defiance of the fact that the productivity of Canadian industry, though increasing faster than American, is still considerably lower.[17] The fact is that only a few unions in Canada have adopted this policy, and those few not at the behest of any American but because their own Canadian members insist that circumstances justify it. In the most conspicuous instance, that of the railway nonoperating unions, where the demand has been made repeatedly, there is every reason to believe that it came perfectly spontaneously from the Canadian membership. Many of them go back and forth across the border in the course of their work, and see their American fellow-workers getting more pay for exactly the same work. Many of them live side by side, in the towns of southern Ontario, with Canadian railway workers working for American lines running through that part of Canada, who get higher pay for exactly the same work. Besides, there was a time, under the McAdoo Award of 1921, when in fact American and Canadian railway workers did get the same rates. It really does not require some evil genius from "outside" to put into the heads of Canadian railwaymen the idea of equal pay for equal work.

There are a few other unions in Canada which have asked for wage parity with the United States. But I think it will be found that in every case they have done so on the ground that the particular Canadian industry concerned was able to afford it.

The railwaymen may, of course, have been wrong. The other unions which have asked for wage parity may have been wrong too. Or they may have been right. That is not the point. The point is

[15] *Op. cit.*, p. 212. The authors note "exceptions" where "American control over the conduct of the negotiations is virtually complete." But they insist they are "exceptional cases."

[16] *Ibid.*

[17] *Ibid.*, Appendices F and G, pp. 333-342.

that they took up the position they did not because some American put them up to it, or because of some international union iron law that Canadian wages must equal American, but for purely Canadian reasons: because they, the Canadian workers concerned, thought they were entitled to the same wages as their American fellows, and thought the Canadian employers concerned were able to pay them.

Canadian unionists certainly want to narrow the gap between Canadian wages and American. Why not? If Canadian productivity is rising faster, surely the gap ought to narrow.

Brecher and Reisman give figures, for manufacturing industries, which show that in fact it has narrowed considerably. In 1939, average hourly earnings in American manufacturing were 53.1 per cent higher than in Canadian manufacturing; by 1950 the differential had shrunk to 42.1 per cent, and by 1955 to 31.9.[18] By 1957, the differential was only 30.2 per cent, in June, 1958, it was only 26.8. (See Appendix Table 23.) (This last abrupt change, however, probably only reflects the fact that the Canadian recession has been much less severe than the American.)[19] The narrowing of the gap has not been continuous; it has of course varied from industry to industry; but it is unmistakable.

What did it? Brecher and Reisman say flatly that

It seems reasonable to attribute the relative improvement in Canadian wages primarily to this narrowing of the productivity gap between the two countries. Indeed, the available statistical data, however imperfect and incomplete, lend no support to the view that the relative wage improvement in Canada has been any greater than can be accounted for by productivity gains in Canada's favour.

Nor is this all. The proposition that productivity changes have been the over-riding consideration . . . would seem to be fully consistent with the evidence that has been gathered on the pattern of collective bargaining in this country. This evidence shows that, in general Canadian locals of international unions, like all labour unions, look chiefly to such factors as the employer's ability to pay, wage rates in other Canadian regions and in-

[18] *Op. cit.*, Table 33, p. 217; Appendix E, pp. 316-332, gives figures for agricultural implements, chemical products, electrical apparatus and supplies, motor vehicles, primary iron and steel, pulp and paper, and textiles.

[19] There are no Canadian figures of straight-time hourly earnings. So the comparison must perforce be between gross hourly earnings, including overtime in the two countries. The greater severity of the recession in the United States has, of course, meant a bigger cut in overtime there than in Canada. In June, 1958, average gross hourly earnings in Canada were 4.0 per cent higher than the year before; in the United States, the increase was only 2.4 per cent.

dustries, increased mechanization, the over-all level of employment and changes in the cost of living.   All of these criteria are weighed in the light of the central consideration that the union seeks to achieve its objective to the fullest extent possible without bargaining its members out of their jobs. . . .

This is not to say that international unions do not cite the Canada-United States wage differential in the course of their negotiations.   On the contrary, . . . they frequently make pointed reference to wages and other benefits prevailing in the United States.   Typically, however, this would seem to be in the nature of an expendable supporting argument which is rarely pursued in the critical stages of collective bargaining.   Cases have, of course, arisen where wage parity with the United States has been sought as an important objective, but often on the ground that such demands are justified by the fact that productivity in Canada was no lower than that in the United States.   It is significant, moreover, . . . that where reference is made to the wage differential, the initiative would seem to come from the Canadian side, not from international headquarters; and that this negotiating technique is used not only by international unions but by purely Canadian unions as well. . . .

There is little evidence to suggest that the expansion of Canadian industry has been impeded by international union extraction of excessive returns to labour; or that the pattern of wage results achieved by these organizations differs in any significant degree from those of the purely Canadian unions.[20]

I have quoted this passage at some length even though some of it only repeats what I have already said myself.   I have done so deliberately.   The trade union civil servant, however objective he tries to be, is inevitably open to suspicion of *déformation professionelle*.   But here are two independent scholars, employed by a Royal Commission, and enjoying ample facilities for a far more exhaustive investigation than any union research director; and they have come to substantially the same conclusions.

VI

Three further comments on the autonomy of Canadian sections of international unions are perhaps in order.   One is that many Canadian unions have, of their own free will, given up their identity and gone into international unions.   A second is that nearly half the membership of purely Canadian unions is now affiliated with the

[20] *Ibid.*, pp. 217-220.

CLC, and hence closely associated with the international unions. A third, perhaps the most significant of all, is that the Canadian and Catholic Confederation of Labour, once fiercely nationalist, and only three years ago severely critical of the proposed CLC on the ground that it and its unions were still really American "colonies," has now twice voted to affiliate with that same CLC, and is negotiating for admission. Very few Canadian unionists indeed now want to isolate themselves from, let alone oppose, international unionism. The proof of the pudding is in the eating. Canadian workers, after sampling various rival confections, seem to find this one both palatable and digestible. They are presumably as good judges of their own economic health as the employers and publicists who, from time to time, burst into speech and print to denounce this diet and prescribe a very different one.

I am not quite certain whether the title of this paper is intended to cover not only the sort of thing I have been discussing but also the influence of American policies in general, American public policy and legislation, on Canadian labor. If so, I am afraid I must plead ignorance as my excuse for any but a very cursory treatment. Obviously, American tariff and trade policies affect Canadian industry, and therefore Canadian labor, profoundly. Obviously also, what the American Administration and Congress do to prevent or stop recessions affects Canadian industry, and therefore Canadian labor, profoundly. Further, American labor legislation affects Canadian; for example, the whole idea of making collective bargaining compulsory by law is American; and the various State "right-to-work" acts, with the disclosures of the McLellan Committee, have given Canadian employers several sticks with which to beat Canadian unions. But, on the other hand, Canadian collective bargaining acts are by no means copies of the Wagner Act; Canada has had no Taft-Hartley Act and has so far no "right-to-work" acts; and Canada has not copied most of the American social security legislation, but has taken a completely different line. Even the current Canadian investigation of the American old age security plan is inspired more by a feeling that our own, though indispensable, is inadequate, than by any feeling that we simply must have the latest thing (not very late at that) from Washington.

Generally speaking, American labor and social legislation has not had much influence on Canadian unions except as something to be avoided. In most cases, we think our own is better.

One of the very marked differences between American and Canadian labor is that American labor leaders, without exception as far as I can recall, constantly profess an ardent devotion to "free enterprise"; whereas even the most conservative Canadian labor leaders hardly ever mention the phrase. This is partly ingrained British distrust of doctrinaire attitudes, partly the Labour party and co-operative heritage brought over by British working-class immigrants in their baggage, partly Roman Catholic suspicion of "economic liberalism," partly the native Canadian tradition of public ownership. After all, our central bank, almost half of our electric power industry, half our railways, our wheat-selling agency, the central core of our radio and television system, our transcontinental air service, our synthetic rubber industry, and a variety of other things are publicly owned, and much of this public ownership is the work of the Conservative party. So any labor leader who started singing the praises of "free enterprise" and supporting or opposing particular measures or policies on the basis of their consonance with, or dissonance from, that dogma, would look pretty silly and would certainly get a very cool reception from the mass of union members. This does not mean that most Canadian labor leaders are socialists. Some of them are, and some of the most prominent. For instance, one of the two Executive Vice-Presidents of the Canadian Labour Congress is Vice-President of the CCF, and has only just ended a period of seventeen years as a CCF Member of Parliament and several years as Deputy Leader; the other Executive Vice-President is an active member of the CCF and has repeatedly been a CCF candidate for Parliament; and the fourth executive officer, the Secretary-Treasurer, is a former Leader of the CCF in the Nova Scotia Legislature. This, of course, does not mean that the CLC is CCF. But it plainly does mean that active membership in a socialist party is no bar to high office in the union movement. On the other hand, the results of the last Dominion general election, when the CCF vote from all classes was only about half the number of union members, and CCF candidates captured hardly any of the industrial seats, show equally plainly that the bulk of Canadian unionists are far from being ardent socialists. Most of them probably are reasonably content with the existing mixed Canadian economic system: private enterprise plus public ownership plus co-operative ownership plus government planning through the central bank and the tariff and taxation and social welfare. They might like to have rather more of some of the ingredients, rather less of others; but they seem as little stirred by trumpet calls to support "free enterprise" as by clarion blasts to get rid of it. So this is one place where American influence seems to have made no impression whatever.

Where it has made an impression, its effect has been, as might be expected, almost invariably conservative, certainly in recent years. It used to be a central and cherished part of the folklore of Canadian employers that Canadian workers were peaceful, docile, other-worldly people, who would never think of asking for higher wages or shorter hours if some wild-eyed American "agitator" or "walking delegate" didn't put them up to it; from which, of course, it followed that purely Canadian unions would present no difficulties. Sad experience has now convinced most Canadian employers that this is an illusion. Quebec employers particularly, who at one time smiled fondly on the purely Canadian Catholic unions, now are more inclined to pray for the day when those nice, quiet, peaceable, reasonable international unions will take over. This is, of course, an oversimplification; but there is no doubt that American influence is, and is now generally recognized to be, a restraining rather than an inflaming influence. International headquarters is much more likely to discourage strikes than to encourage them, for the excellent reason that it has to foot the bill, or most of it, and union treasurers are no more enthusiastic about drawing down their balances than any other treasurers. Their attitude is pretty certain to be: "Is your journey really necessary?"

To sum up: Canadian labor is profoundly influenced by American labor organizations and policies. It always has been. It always will be. It has drawn heavily upon American money, American staff, American know-how, American experience. It still does, but much less than it used to, and less and less every year. It is now strong enough to build up considerable funds of its own. It no longer needs American staff or American know-how, except in very special cases and then only temporarily. Canadian business, on the other hand, especially in certain key sectors, is just as dependent as ever, or more so, on American capital, American technology, American managerial know-how. Hence the contrast between increasing American influence in Canadian business and decreasing American influence in Canadian labor.

It must be emphasized, however, that even the international unions in Canada have also always drawn considerably on British experience, British staff, British know-how: some of the ablest, most successful and most prominent Canadian union leaders, even in recent years, have been Old Country men; and a Clydeside accent is still common at CLC conventions, and a not inconsiderable asset to its possessor. There is also, even in the international unions, a strong, healthy Canadian nationalism. The CLC of today is proud to trace its direct and unbroken descent from the Canadian Labor Congress of 1883. Canadian unionists are proud of the TLC's long struggle to establish its complete autonomy, its equality with the AFL. They are jealous of the autonomy and equality which now exists between the CLC and the AFL-CIO, and of the autonomy of the Canadian sections of international unions. They will defend it against any encroachments.

This does not mean that Canadian labor is anti-American. On the contrary, its relations with American labor are close and cordial, and certain to remain so. The two movements are inextricably bound together by all the ties which bind the two countries together, and by special, organizational ties as well. They are, like the nations of the British Commonwealth, "in no way subordinate one to another in any aspect of their domestic or external affairs," though united by the fact that most of their constituent unions are affiliated with the AFL-CIO in the United States for their American membership, and with the CLC in Canada for their Canadian membership; and the two movements are also, of course, freely associated, with the other central labor organizations of the free world, in the International Confederation of Free Trade Unions. The analogy with the Commonwealth must not, of course, be pushed too far. Analogies in political or economic discussion are always dangerous. I have, nonetheless, used this analogy deliberately, because I think the relationship between the American and Canadian labor movements is, like the relationship between the nations of the Commonwealth, real, important, complex, hard to define, constantly changing, easily comprehended by those who live in it, often an impenetrable mystery to those who do not.

cies in Canadian labor, and deepening American influence in Canadian labor.

It must be emphasized, however, that even the international
unions in Canada have also always drawn considerably on British
experience. British still British know-how, some of the ablest, most
successful and most prominent Canadian union leaders, even in
recent years, have been Old Country men, and a Old Country accent
in the councils of CLC conventions, and a more incongruous used
as its postscript. There it also, even in the internal influence, a
strong tradition Canadian-nationalism. Thus CLC officials, as usual
to take as direct and subject to dissent from the Canadian labor
Congress of the general in principle, are point of the TUC and
certain British unions to continue autonomy, to usually act as
go-between the CLC and the AFL-CIO, and in the question of
the Canadian relation of international unions. They were defined in
terms the essentially the

This does not mean that Canadian labor is anti-American. On the
contrary the relation with American labor are close and cordial, and
certain common The two movements are peaceful and bound to
gather in all respects, when hand the two nations, are a whole, so
mutual organizations means well. However like the interest of
the British Commonwealth, who in most an order to the general
in support of their "unreal" or cordial aid and close coordinated
to the and the world that to cooperation unions the affiliate with the
AFL-CIO in the United States are close and closely developing and
still the CLC in Canada for those Canadian membership, and the
two movements acting close one of clearly associated with the other
central labor organization of the free world. In no true, for mutual
Confederation of Free Labor Union. Understandably with this Cana-
more with more one, of course, is gained too far an indispensable only
to no complete distribution are close arguments, I have then the
time, and the industry definitely, because I think the relationship
between American and Canadian labor movements, the close co-
laboring between the nations of two Commonwealth, and important enough, more of defies constantly bringing, easily compre-
hensible to those who live in it, often as impenetrable mystery to
those who do.

APPENDIX

TABLE 1
CANADA'S POPULATION AND LABOR FORCE, SELECTED YEARS, 1871-1957
(All figures in thousands)

| Year | Total Population | DISTRIBUTION (Percentages) | | | CIVILIAN LABOR FORCE | | | | |
| | | Urban | Rural | Total | Employed | | | | Seeking work |
					Non-Agri.	Agri-cultural	Total		
1871	3,689	19.5	80.5						
1881	4,325	25.6	74.4						
1891	4,833	31.8	68.2						
1901	5,371	37.5	62.5						
1911	7,207	45.4	54.6						
1921	8,788	49.5	50.5						
1931	10,377	53.7	46.3	4,105	2,427	1,203	3,630		475
1935	10,845			4,354	2,452	1,284	3,736		618
1939	11,267			4,598	2,711	1,364	4,075		523
1941	11,507	54.4	45.6	4,417	3,014	1,210	4,224		193
1946	12,292			4,862	3,467	1,271	4,738		124
1951	14,009	62.9	37.1	5,236	4,164	991	5,155		81
1953	14,781			5,380	4,368	897	5,265		115
1955	15,601			5,537	4,451	873	5,324		213
1956	16,081	66.7	33.3	5,705	4,752	773	5,526		179
1957	16,589			5,915	4,915	745	5,661		254

Sources: Census of Canada, 1951 and 1956; Canada Year Book, 1956; Canadian Statistical Review.

TABLE 2

INDUSTRIAL DISTRIBUTION OF THE CIVILIAN LABOR FORCE IN CANADA
(Averages for Selected Years, 1927-1955)

	1927-29	1937-39	1947-49	1953-55
	(Thousands)			
Agriculture	1,217	1,274	1,099	849
Total Business	2,193	2,382	3,309	3,775
Resource Industries	202	227	223	273
Manufacturing	740	729	1,285	1,354
Construction	175	194	288	351
Transportation, Storage, and Communication	301	249	371	406
Trade, Finance, and Services	775	982	1,143	1,392
Civilian Government and Community Services	263	313	484	631
Totals	3,675	3,969	4,893	5,256
	(Percentage)			
Agriculture	33.1	33.2	22.5	16.2
Total Business	59.7	59.9	67.6	71.8
Resource Industries	5.5	5.7	4.6	5.2
Manufacturing	20.1	18.3	26.2	25.8
Construction	4.8	4.9	5.9	6.7
Transportation, Storage, and Communications	8.2	6.3	7.6	7.7
Trade, Finance, and Services	21.1	24.7	23.4	26.5
Civilian Government and Community Services	7.2	7.9	9.9	12.0
Totals	100.0	100.0	100.0	100.0

Details do not always add to totals because of rounding.
Source: Royal Commission on Canadian Economic Prospects, *Final Report*, p. 364.

TABLE 3
INDUSTRIAL DISTRIBUTION OF CANADA'S GROSS DOMESTIC OUTPUT
(Averages for Selected Years, 1927-1955)

	1927-29	1937-39	1947-49	1953-55
	(Billions of 1949 Dollars)			
Agriculture	2.01	1.85	1.89	2.22
Total Business	5.80	5.80	10.40	13.45
Resource Industries	0.55	0.77	1.04	1.64
Manufacturing	1.87	2.09	4.12	5.13
Construction	0.49	0.38	0.75	1.10
Transportation, Storage, and Communications	0.76	0.61	1.18	1.44
Trade, Finance, and Services	2.12	1.95	3.31	4.13
Civilian Government and Community Services	0.78	0.92	1.41	1.77
Total	8.58	8.57	13.70	17.44
	(Percentage)			
Agriculture	23.4	21.6	13.8	12.7
Total Business	67.6	67.7	75.9	77.1
Resource Industries	6.4	9.0	7.6	9.4
Manufacturing	21.8	24.4	30.1	29.5
Construction	5.7	4.4	5.5	6.3
Transportation, Storage and Communications	8.9	7.1	8.6	8.3
Trade, Finance, and Services	24.8	22.7	24.2	23.6
Civilian Government and Community Services	9.0	10.7	10.3	10.2
Total	100.0	100.0	100.0	100.0

Details may not add to total because of rounding.
Source: Royal Commission on Canada's Economic Prospect, *Final Report*, p. 357.

TABLE 4

GROSS NATIONAL PRODUCT AND INDEXES OF INDUSTRIAL PRODUCTION
IN CANADA AND THE UNITED STATES, 1929-1957
(Five-Year Averages, 1930-1950; Annual, 1950-1957)

Year or Period	INDUSTRIAL PRODUCTION (1947-1949 = 100)		GROSS NATIONAL PRODUCT (Billions of current dollars)	
	Canada	United States	Canada $ Can.	United States $ U. S.
1929	53	59	6.2	104
1930-34	39	39	4.3	69
1935-39	51	54	5.1	85
1940-44	93	102	9.8	158
1945-49	97	100	13.9	235
1950	109	112	18.0	285
1951	116	120	21.5	329
1952	119	124	23.3	347
1953	128	134	24.4	365
1954	126	125	24.0	363
1955	136	139	26.8	397
1956	146	143	30.0	419
1957	146	143	31.1	440

Note: The Canadian index of industrial production was converted from its base of 1935-1939 to the 1947-1949 base by the editor.
Sources: Industrial Production: Canada, 1920-1934 and 1951-1955, Brecher and Reisman, *Canada-United States Economic Relations*, pp. 247, 266; 1935-1950, Dominion Bureau of Statistics; United States: *Federal Reserve Bulletin* Gross National Product: Canada, Dominion Bureau of Statistics; United States, U. S. Department of Commerce.

TABLE 5
COMPARATIVE ECONOMIC POSITION OF CANADA RELATIVE TO THE UNITED STATES IN 1955

Economic Indicator	Canada	United States	Differential: Canada as percentage of United States
Population (millions)	15.6	165.2	9.3
Labor Force (incl. armed forces—millions)	5.68	68.9	8.2
GNP:	(Can. $)	(U. S. $)	
Total (billions $ 1949)	21.6	344	6.3
Total (billions $ current)	26.8	391	6.8
Per Capita ($ 1949)	1384	2081	66.5
Per Capita ($ current)	1719	2366	72.7
Per Worker ($ 1949)	3801	4990	76.2
Per Worker ($ current)	4716	5673	83.1
Disposable Personal Income:	(Can. $)	(U. S. $)	
Total (billions $ current)	18.2	270.6	6.7
Per Capita ($ current)	1168.7	1637	71.4
Per Worker ($ current)	3206.5	3927	81.7
Personal Consumption Expenditures:	(Can. $)	(U. S. $)	
Total (billions $ 1949)	14.3	226	6.3
Total (billions $ current)	16.9	254	6.6
Per Capita ($ 1949)	918.3	1366	67.2
Per Capita ($ current)	1084	1537	70.5
Per Worker ($ 1949)	2519.4	3274	76.9
Per Worker ($ current)	2975	3686	80.7
Average hours per week:			
Manufacturing—annual average	41.0	40.7	100.7
Manufacturing—selected week	41.5	41.1	101.0
Non-agricultural—private sector	41.3	38.9	106.2
Wage Rates—manufacturing:	(Can. c.)	(U. S. c.)	
Average hourly	144.8	191.0	75.8
	(Can. $)	(U. S. $)	
Average weekly	59.25	76.52	75.8
Output per man-hour ($ 1949)	(Can. $)	(U. S. $)	
Total Private Sector—GNP	1.83	2.49	73.3

Source: Brecher and Reisman, *Canada-United States Economic Relations,* p. 224.

TABLE 6
Trade of Canada with Various Countries, Selected Years, 1886-1955

	Year	Total ($ millions)	PERCENTAGE OF TOTAL WITH:			
			U. S.	U. K.	Other C'wealth Countries	Other Countries
Imports	1886	96.0	44.6	40.7	2.5	12.2
	1901	177.9	60.3	24.1	2.2	13.4
	1911	452.6	60.8	24.3	4.4	10.5
	1921	1,247.2	69.0	17.3	4.2	9.5
	1926	1,008.3	66.3	16.3	5.0	12.4
	1929	1,299.0	68.8	15.0	4.8	11.4
	1937	808.9	60.7	18.2	11.0	10.1
	1939	751.1	66.1	15.2	10.0	8.7
	1947	2,574.0	76.7	7.4	6.5	9.5
	1950	3,174.3	67.1	12.7	7.6	12.6
	1952	4,030.5	73.9	8.9	4.6	12.6
	1953	4,382.9	73.5	10.3	3.9	12.3
	1954	4,093.3	72.4	9.6	4.4	13.6
	1955	4,711.7	73.3	8.5	4.4	13.8
Exports	1886	77.8	44.1	47.2	4.2	4.5
	1901	177.5	38.3	52.3	4.5	4.9
	1911	274.3	38.0	48.2	6.1	7.7
	1921	1,189.1	45.6	26.3	7.6	20.5
	1926	1,261.2	36.3	36.4	7.6	19.7
	1929	1,152.4	42.8	25.2	9.1	22.9
	1937	997.4	36.1	40.3	10.4	13.2
	1939	924.9	41.1	35.5	11.1	12.3
	1947	2,774.9	37.3	27.1	15.0	20.6
	1950	3,118.4	64.8	15.1	5.9	14.2
	1952	4,301.1	53.7	17.3	6.1	22.9
	1953	4,117.4	58.7	16.2	5.6	19.5
	1954	3,881.4	59.7	16.9	5.0	18.4
	1955	4,281.7	59.8	18.0	5.5	16.7

Source: *Canada Year Book,* 1956, p. 968.

TABLE 7
CANADIAN EXPORTS AND IMPORTS AS PERCENTAGES OF GROSS AVAILABLE SUPPLY,[a] SELECTED YEARS, 1926-1954
(Based on current dollars)

	EXPORTS		IMPORTS	
Year	Total	To U. S.	Total	From U. S.
1926	24.2	11.5	22.3	14.9
1929	20.1	11.1	24.0	16.5
1932	17.2	9.0	19.3	12.6
1935	21.3	11.2	19.0	11.8
1938	20.9	10.2	19.4	12.5
1941	23.5	10.0	18.8	13.0
1944	22.9	13.1	23.0	12.9
1947	20.9	9.8	20.8	16.4
1950	18.7	12.7	19.9	14.4
1951	18.8	11.7	20.7	15.2
1952	19.4	11.4	18.8	14.4
1953	17.8	11.4	19.3	14.4
1954	17.3	11.2	18.8	13.9

[a] Gross available supply equals gross national product plus imports of goods and services.
Source: Brecher and Reisman, *Canada-United States Economic Relations*, pp. 67, 73.

TABLE 8
THE CHANGING ROLE OF THE UNITED STATES AND THE UNITED KINGDOM IN CANADIAN TRADE AND INVESTMENT
(In Percentages)

Year	MERCHANDISE EXPORTS		TOTAL CURRENT RECEIPTS		MERCHANDISE IMPORTS		NONRESIDENT INVESTMENT		ANNUAL INFLOWS OF DIRECT INVESTMENT [a]	
	U. S.	U. K.	U. S.	U. K.	U. S.	U. K.	U. S.	U. K.	U. S.	U. K.
1926	36.3	36.4	47.3	21.1	66.3	16.3	53.3	43.3	73.7	26.3
1930	43.2	27.2	56.7	15.7	64.8	16.1	60.5	36.8	100.0	0.0
1939	41.1	35.5	53.5	26.4	66.2	15.2	60.9	36.2	....	....
1945	32.6	40.9[b]	39.1	37.5[b]	75.8	8.9	70.4	25.4	95.0	5.0
1948	48.8	22.2	54.2	22.2	68.5	11.4	74.7	21.3	85.9	14.1
1952	53.6	17.3	56.2	15.7	73.9	8.9	78.4	17.6	92.2	4.2

[a] The first and third annual inflow ratios relate to 1927 and 1946 rather than 1926 and 1945. No figures are available for 1926, 1939, and 1945. For 1948 and 1952 the United Kingdom ratio includes all countries in the sterling area.
[b] Canadian current-account credits with the United Kingdom in 1945 include mutual aid and other financial assistance valued at $596 millions, or about 36% of total current credits with that country.
Source: Brecher and Reisman, *Canada-United States Economic Relations*, p. 49.

TABLE 9
Nonresident Long-Term Investment in Canada, Selected Years, 1900-1957

| End of Year | Amount ($ millions) Owned by Residents of | | | | Percentage of Totals | | |
	U. S.	U. K.	Other Countries	Total	U. S.	U. K.	Other
1900	168	1,050	14	1,232	14	85	1
1914	881	2,778	178	3,837	23	72	5
1918	1,630	2,729	177	4,536	36	60	4
1926	3,196	2,637	170	6,003	53	44	3
1930	4,660	2,766	188	7,614	61	36	3
1939	4,151	2,476	286	6,913	60	36	4
1945	4,990	1,750	352	7,092	70	25	5
1949	5,906	1,717	340	7,963	74	22	4
1953	8,870	2,008	583	11,461	77	18	5
1954	9,692	2,181	704	12,577	77	17	6
1955	10,289	2,347	832	13,468	77	17	6
1956	11,651	2,675	1,075	15,400	76	17	7
1957	13,035	2,910	1,255	17,200	76	17	7

Note: Figures for 1900 from a study by Dr. Jacob Viner, for 1914 and 1918 from work of Prof. F. A. Knox, and for 1926 to 1956 from the Dominion Bureau of Statistics (especially *Canada's International Investment Position 1926-54* and *The Canadian Balance of International Payments, 1956*). Figures for 1957 are estimated by The Bank of Nova Scotia. Investments shown for U. S. and U. K. include some held for residents of other countries. Offsetting the $17,200 millions of long-term foreign Investment in Canada in 1957, Canadian residents held close to $5 billions in long-term investments abroad; when account is taken of the official exchange reserves and certain other items, the balance of Canada's foreign indebtedness is of the order of $11 billions.

Source: The Bank of Nova Scotia, *Monthly Bulletin*, March, 1958.

TABLE 10
NATURE OF FOREIGN INVESTMENT IN CANADA, SELECTED YEARS, 1930-1955
(Amounts for end of year in $ millions)

	1930	1939	1945	1949	1955	1956	1957
United States, Direct	1,993	1,881	2,304	3,095	6,517	7,425	8,225
United States, Other	2,667	2,270	2,686	2,811	3,772	4,226	4,810
Total United States	4,660	4,151	4,990	5,906	10,289	11,561	13,035
United Kingdom, Direct	392	366	348	428	883	1,057	1,175
United Kingdom, Other	2,374	2,110	1,402	1,289	1,464	1,618	1,735
Others, Direct	42	49	61	63	315	418	500
Others, Other	146	237	291	277	517	657	755
Total Overseas	2,954	2,762	2,102	2,057	3,179	3,750	4,165
Total	7,614	6,913	7,092	7,963	13,468	15,400	17,200

Note: D. B. S. figures for 1930 to 1956. Figures for 1957 estimated by the Bank of Nova Scotia.
Source: The Bank of Nova Scotia, *Monthly Bulletin*, March, 1958.

TABLE 11

PERCENTAGES OF VARIOUS SECTORS OF CANADIAN INDUSTRY OWNED
AND CONTROLLED BY NONRESIDENTS; SELECTED YEAR ENDS,
1926-1954

	OWNED						CONTROLLED					
	1926	1930	1939	1948	1953	1954	1926	1930	1939	1948	1953	1954
By all nonresidents:												
Manufacturing[a]	38	40	42	42	47	48	35	36	38	43	51	54
Mining, Smelting,												
Petro. Explor.[a]	37	44	40	39	56	59	38	47	42	40	57	59
Railways	55	56	57	45	37	35	3	3	3	3	2	2
Other Utilities	32	36	27	20	17	16	20	29	26	24	12	11
Above Industries plus												
Merchandising and												
Construction	37	39	38	32	32	32	17	20	21	25	28	28
By U. S. Residents:												
Manufacturing[a]	30	33	34	35	38	39	30	31	32	39	44	45
Mining, Smelting, and												
Petro. Explor.[a]	28	34	31	32	52	54	32	42	38	37	55	57
Railways	15	21	18	21	16	16	3	3	3	3	2	2
Other Utilities	23	30	20	16	15	14	20	29	26	24	11	10
Above Industries plus												
Merchandising and												
Construction	19	24	22	23	25	25	15	18	19	22	24	25

[a] Investments in exploration and development of petroleum by companies engaged principally in refining and production of petroleum products are included in manufacturing.

Source: Brecher and Reisman, *Canada-United States Economic Relations*, pp. 100-101.

TABLE 12

CANADA'S BALANCE OF INTERNATIONAL INDEBTEDNESS,
SELECTED YEAR ENDS, 1926-1955[a]

(Billions of Canadian dollars)

Item	1926	1930	1933	1939	1945	1948	1954	1955
Canadian liabilities:								
Foreign long-term capital invested in Canada	6.0	7.6	7.4	6.9	7.1	7.5	12.6	13.5
Other liabilities	0.4	0.4	0.3	0.5	0.5	0.9	1.1	1.2
Total liabilities	6.4	8.0	7.7	7.4	7.6	8.4	13.7	14.8
Canadian assets:								
Canadian long-term capital invested abroad	0.9	1.3	1.3	1.4	2.0	3.6	4.6	4.8
Other assets	0.4	0.2	0.1	0.5	1.8	1.0	2.3	2.2
Total assets	1.3	1.5	1.4	1.9	3.8	4.7	6.9	6.9
Net international indebtedness	5.1	6.5	6.3	5.5	3.9	3.7	6.8	7.8

[a] Exclusive of short-term commercial indebtedness and blocked currencies.
Details may not add to totals because of rounding.
Source: Brecher and Reisman, *Canada-United States Economic Relations*, p. 86.

TABLE 13

THE CANADIAN BALANCE OF INTERNATIONAL PAYMENTS, 1926-1950

(Five-year annual averages; millions of Canadian dollars. All figures are positive unless preceded by a minus sign.)

Geographical Region	1926-30	1931-35	1936-40	1941-45	1946-50
United States					
Current receipts	822	503	764	1637	2134
Current payments	1144	622	891	1727	2761
Balance	− 322	−119	−127	− 90	− 627
United Kingdom					
Current receipts	288	223	447	1675	843
Current payments	325	210	274	755	425
Balance	− 37	13	173	920	418
Other Countries					
Current receipts	496	228	311	471	1052
Current payments	249	138	199	228	601
Balance	247	90	112	243	451
All Countries					
Current receipts	1606	955	1523	3782	3929
Current payments	1718	971	1364	2710	3754
Balance	112	− 16	159	1072	175
Official contributions	..	..	..	668	34
Net capital movements	138[a]	− 1	− 169	− 404	− 141

[a] Average of four years, 1927-30.

Sources: Bank of Canada, *Statistical Summary, 1950 Supplement*, p. 125; Dominion Bureau of Statistics, *The Canadian Balance of International Payments, 1955.*

TABLE 14

THE CANADIAN BALANCE OF INTERNATIONAL PAYMENTS, 1951-1956
(In millions of Canadian dollars; all figures are positive unless preceded by a minus sign)

Geographical Region	1951	1952	1953	1954	1955	1956
United States						
Current receipts	3178	3274	3443	3306	3696	3998
Current payments	4129	4123	4347	4113	4737	5368
Balance	− 951	− 849	− 904	− 807	−1041	−1640
Net capital movement	515	− 158	244	277	405	936
United Kingdom						
Current receipts	821	925	830	836	980	1014
Current payments	598	537	697	607	639	760
Balance	223	388	133	229	341	254
Other Countries						
Current receipts	1312	1659	1464	1378	1385	1582
Current payments	1092	1018	1111	1221	1353	1838
Balance	220	641	353	157	32	− 256
All Countries						
Current receipts	5311	5858	5737	5520	6061	6594
Current payments	5819	5678	6155	5941	6729	7936
Balance	− 508	180	− 418	− 421	− 668	−1342
Official contributions	9	16	25	11	24	30
Net capital movement	517	− 164	443	432	692	1372

Sources: Dominion Bureau of Statistics, *The Canadian Balance of International Payments* (Issues for 1955, 1956, and 1957).

TABLE 16
SEEDED ACREAGE AND YIELD OF WHEAT, CANADA AND THE
UNITED STATES, 1925-1957

Year	UNITED STATES		CANADA	
	Seeded Acreage Million Acres	Yield Bushels per acre	Seeded Acreage Million Acres	Yield Bushels per acre
1925-29	58.2	12.6	23.1	19.5
1930	66.7	11.0	25.7	13.6
1935-39	73.2	10.4	25.6	12.2
1940-44	59.9	15.4	22.3	18.9
1945-49	76.3	15.8	24.6	14.8
1949	83.9	13.1	27.9	12.9
1950	71.3	14.3	27.3	17.1
1951	78.5	12.6	25.3	21.9
1952	78.6	16.6	26.2	26.8
1953	78.9	14.9	26.4	24.0
1954	62.5	15.7	25.5	13.0
1955	58.2	16.0	22.7	22.9
1956	60.7	16.6	22.8	25.2
1957	49.9	19.0	21.0	17.6

Sources: *Dominion Bureau of Statistics*, Handbook of Agricultural Statistics and Supplements; U. S. Deptartment of Agriculture, *Agricultural Statistics*, 1956 and earlier years.

TABLE 15
COMPARATIVE WHEAT PRICES, CANADA AND THE UNITED STATES, 1938-1957
(Dollars per bushel Domestic Currency)

Crop of	UNITED STATES		CANADA		E:
	Support Price as Percentage of Parity	Price Received by Farmer	Price to Farmer No. 1 Northern at Ft. William	Average Farm Price	
1938	52	$ .56	$ .80	$ .58	
1939	56	.69	.70	.53	
1940	57	.67	.76	.57	
1941	85	.94	.85	.59	
1942	85	1.09	1.02	.76	
1943	85	1.35	1.37	1.13	
1944	90	1.41	1.44	1.25	
1945	90	1.49	1.83	1.64	
1946	90	1.90	1.83	1.62	
1947	90	2.29	1.83	1.63	
1948	90	1.98	1.83	1.63	
1949	90	1.88	1.83	1.60	
1950	90	2.00	1.86	1.52	
1951	90	2.11	1.84	1.58	
1952	90	2.09	1.82	1.58	
1953	91	2.04	1.56	1.32	
1954	90	2.12	1.65	1.45[a]	
1955	82.5	1.98	1.61	1.41[a]	
1956	82.6	1.97	1.59	1.39[a]	
1957	82.5	1.94			

[a] Estimated (Price at Fort William less 20 cents).
Source: *Price Programs* U. S. D. A.; Annual Reports of Canadian Wheat Board; *Agricultural Statistics,* Dominion Bureau of Statistics.

TABLE 17

SUPPLY AND DISAPPEARANCE OF WHEAT, UNITED STATES, FIVE-YEAR
AVERAGES, 1930-1949, ANNUAL, 1950-1958

(Million bushels)

Year beginning July 1	SUPPLY				DISAPPEARANCE		
	Carry-over, July 1	Produc-tion	Imports	Total[a]	Domestic	Exports	Total
1930-34 Average	325.9	732.5	3.0	1,061.4	703.5	60.8	764.3
1935-39 "	154.5	758.6	14.2	927.3	688.8	53.3	742.1
1940-44 "	446.1	926.0	37.5	1,409.6	908.2	55.3	963.5
1945-49 "	193.3	1,202.4	1.2	1,396.9	759.1	415.4	1,174.5
1950	424.7	1,019.3	11.9	1,456.0	690.0	366.1	1,056.1
1951	399.9	988.2	31.6	1,419.6	688.4	475.3	1,163.7
1952	256.0	1,306.4	21.6	1,584.0	660.7	317.8	978.5
1953	605.5	1,173.1	5.5	1,784.2	633.6	217.0	850.6
1954	933.5	983.9	4.2	1,921.6	611.0	274.4	885.4
1955	1,036.2	934.7	9.9	1,980.8	601.1	346.3	947.4
1956	1,033.4	1,004.3	7.7	2,045.3	587.5	549.2	1,136.6
1957 Prelim.	909	947	10	1,866	586	390	976
1958 Projected	890	1,271	5	2,166	593	375	968

[a]Due to rounding, items do not always add to total.

Source: "The Wheat Situation," Agricultural Marketing Service, U. S. D. A.

TABLE 18

SUPPLY AND DISAPPEARANCE OF WHEAT, CANADA, FIVE-YEAR
AVERAGES, 1930-1949, ANNUAL 1950-1957
(Million bushels)

Crop Year	SUPPLY				DISAPPEARANCE		
	Carryover beginning of crop yr.	Production	Imports	Total[a]	Domestic	Exports	Total
1930-34 average	164.3	348.6		513.3	113.4	218.1	331.5
1935-39 "	101.1	312.4		415.4	114.4	182.5	296.9
1940-44 "	431.1	421.6		852.9	158.6	271.7	430.3
1945-49 "	119.6	362.8		482.6	145.2	274.0	392.2
1950	112.2	466.5		578.7	148.5	241.0	389.5
1951	189.2	553.6		742.9	169.9	355.8	525.7
1952	217.2	701.9		919.1	150.4	385.5	536.0
1953	383.2	634.0		1,017.6	143.9	255.1	399.0
1954	618.7	332.0		950.8	162.2	251.9	414.1
1955	536.7	519.2		1,056.0	167.2	309.2	476.4
1956	579.6	573.1		1,152.8	161.4	261.8	423.2
1957	729.5	370.5		1,100.1	na	na	na

[a] Includes a minor amount of imports.
na—Not available.
Source: Dominion Bureau of Statistics.

TABLE 19
UNITED STATES AND CANADIAN EXPORTS OF WHEAT AND WHEAT FLOUR, SELECTED COUNTRIES AND YEARS
(Million bushels)

	CROP YEAR									
	1925-29		1945-49		1950-54		1955-56		1956-57	
	U. S.	Canada	U. S.	Canada	U. S.	Canada	U. S.	Canada	U. S.	Canada
United Kingdom	32.2	193.3	14.7	151.0	21.1	107.3	24.9	108.6	39.8	81.0
Benelux	20.5	24.3	31.7	13.3	26.6	25.4	30.7	25.4	39.1	27.8
France	5.2	4.4	18.5	2.0	3.3	1.9	7.9	1.7	30.9	4.0
Germany	6.5	14.2	91.7	1.2	43.1	17.3	16.8	29.6	35.4	36.3
Italy & Trieste	5.9	10.4	43.1	4.7	12.2	9.0	5.2	6.7	9.6	2.4
Greece	4.6	5.0	18.6	1.4	12.3	.3	13.2	.1	18.8	.0
Yugoslovia[a]	—	.0	3.2	.7	14.4	3.8	37.5	.0	36.5	.0
Other Europe	13.3	13.2	54.6	16.0	27.6	24.7	15.2	63.8	29.6	30.7
Africa	1.1	2.3	12.2	14.0	15.0	12.6	30.1	8.2	14.5	2.7
India & Pakistan[a]	—	.2	11.6	8.0	38.7	12.9	13.5	.0	88.9	1.0
Japan	6.4	12.4	38.9	1.0	38.6	22.6	41.0	29.4	49.8	35.1
Other Asia[b]	10.1	11.8	24.9	11.9	26.1	13.9	45.6	10.4	81.1	10.4
Canada	30.2	—	.5	—	.6	—	1.8	—	.3	—
United States	—	8.8	—	6.4	—	19.3	—	8.3	—	7.6
Brazil	3.9	.5	10.5	1.1	13.9	4.7	17.7	—	13.9	—
Cuba	5.4	.3	6.0	.7	4.7	2.3	6.1	.5	7.5	.3
Other America	24.7	7.7	24.7	13.0	31.2	19.8	32.4	15.3	40.7	13.5

[a] Included in residual total for continent.
[b] Includes Oceania.

Source: Adapted from tables appearing in an unpublished manuscript by W. E. Hamilton and W. M. Drummond.

TABLE 20
Union Membership in Canada, 1911-1958

Year	With International Affiliation		Without International Affiliation		Total membership
	Membership	% of total	Membership	% of total	
1911	119,415	89.7	13,717	10.3	133,132
1912	136,389	85.2	23,731	14.8	160,120
1913	149,577	85.1	26,222	14.9	175,799
1914	140,482	84.5	25,681	15.5	166,163
1915	114,722	80.0	28,621	20.0	143,343
1916	129,123	80.5	31,284	19.5	160,407
1917	164,896	80.6	39,734	19.4	204,630
1918	201,432	80.9	47,455	19.1	248,887
1919	260,247	68.8	117,800	31.2	378,047
1920	267,247	71.5	106,595	28.5	373,842
1921	222,896	71.1	90,424	28.9	313,320
1922	206,150	74.5	70,471	25.5	276,621
1923	203,843	73.3	74,249	26.7	278,092
1924	201,981	77.5	58,662	22.5	260,643
1925	172,573	63.7	98,491	36.3	271,064
1926	179,267	65.3	95,337	34.7	274,604
1927	180,755	62.3	109,527	37.7	290,282
1928	186,917	62.2	113,685	37.8	300,602
1929	203,514	63.7	115,962	36.3	319,476
1930	203,478	63.1	118,971	36.9	322,449
1931	188,219	60.6	122,325	39.4	310,544
1932	176,087	62.2	107,009	37.8	283,096
1933	167,719	58.7	118,001	41.3	285,720
1934	161,404	57.4	119,870	42.6	281,274
1935	143,570	51.2	137,078	48.8	280,648
1936	174,769	54.2	147,977	45.8	322,746
1937	217,465	56.7	166,027	43.3	383,492
1938	230,547	60.4	151,098	39.6	381,645
1939	216,661	60.4	142,306	39.6	358,967
1940	226,969	62.7	135,254	37.3	362,223
1941	288,005	62.4	173,676	37.6	461,681
1942	379,004	65.5	199,376	34.5	578,380
1943	425,423	64.0	239,110	36.0	664,533
1944	468,013	64.6	256,175	35.4	724,188
1945	471,047	66.2	240,070	33.8	711,117
1946	573,258	68.9	258,439	31.1	831,697
1947	620,517	68.0	291,607	32.0	912,124
1948	675,044	69.1	302,550	30.9	977,594
1949	712,598	70.9	293,041	29.1	1,005,639
1950-51	725,613	70.5	302,908	29.5	1,028,521
1952	796,016	69.5	350,105	30.5	1,146,121
1953	850,545	69.7	369,169	30.3	1,219,714
1954	904,693	71.4	363,218	28.6	1,267,911
1955	893,838	70.5	374,369	29.5	1,268,207
1956	947,498	70.1	404,154	29.9	1,351,652
1957	990,469	71.5	395,716	28.5	1,386,185
1958	1,062,315	73.1	391,685	26.9	1,454,000

Source: Brecher and Reisman, *op. cit.,* p. 205; figures brought up to date.

TABLE 21
Twenty Largest Canadian Unions, 1957

Union	Membership
Steelworkers of America, United (Int.)	75,000
Carpenters & Joiners of America, United Brotherhood of (Int.)	68,020
Automobile, Aircraft and Agricultural Implement Workers of America, International Union, United (Int.)	60,000
Machinists, International Association of (Int.)	49,423
Woodworkers of America, International (Int.)	43,911
Railway Employees and Other Transport Workers, Canadian Brotherhood of (National)	34,436
Pulp, Sulphite and Paper Mill Workers, International Brotherhood of (Int.)	33,890
Mine, Mill and Smelter Workers, International Union of (Int.)	33,000
Public Employees, National Union of (National)	30,361
Teamsters, Chauffeurs, Warehousemen and Helpers of America, International Brotherhood of (Int.)	29,275
Electrical, Radio and Machine Workers of America, United (Int.)	24,500
Railway Carmen of America, Brotherhood of (Int.)	24,347
Railroad Trainmen, Brotherhood of (Int.)	24,304
Mine Workers of America, United (Int.)	23,604
Electrical Workers, International Brotherhood of (Int.)	23,550
Packinghouse Workers of America, United (Int.)	21,104
Railway and Steamship Clerks, Freight Handlers, Express and Station Employees, Brotherhood of (Int.)	21,061
Maintenance of Way Employees, Brotherhood of (Int.)	20,000
Bâtiment et du bois, Fédération Nationale Catholique des Métiers du (National)	19,104
Public Service Employees, National Union of (National)	18,000

Source: Labour Organization in Canada, 1957 (Department of Labour, Ottawa), pp. 15-20.

TABLE 22
PERCENTAGE OF CANADIAN MEMBERSHIP IN SELECTED INTERNATIONAL UNIONS, 1957

Union	Total Membership (U. S. & Canadian)	Canadian Membership	Percentage
Woodworkers of America, International	98,517	43,911	44.6
Mine, Mill & Smelter Workers, International Union of	100,000	33,000	33.0
Electrical, Radio & Machine Workers of America, United	100,000	24,500	24.5
Broadcast Employees & Technicians, National Assoc. of	5,100	1,202	23.6
Siderographers, International Association of	45	10	22.2
Pulp, Sulphite & Paper Mill Workers, International Brotherhood of	165,000	33,890	20.5
Railway Carmen of America, Brotherhood of	129,804	24,347	18.8
Commercial Telegraphers' Union, The	32,000	5,341	16.7
Tobacco Workers' International Union	34,686	5,654	16.3
Chemical Workers' Union, International	84,299	13,300	15.8
Locomotive Engineers, Brotherhood of	52,821	8,293	15.7
Railroad Telegraphers, The Order of	65,267	10,201	15.6
Air Line Dispatchers' Association, Canadian	550	81	14.7
Packinghouse Workers of America, United	150,000	21,104	14.1
Seafarers' International Union of North America	75,000	10,450	13.9
Distillery, Rectifying, Wine & Allied Workers' Internat. Union of America	25,000	3,300	13.2
Printers Die Stampers & Engravers' Union of North America, International Plate	800	100	12.5
Longshoremen's Association, International	52,000	6,000	11.5
Railroad Trainmen, Brotherhood of	217,462	24,304	11.2
Locomotive Firemen & Enginemen, Brotherhood of	97,000	10,603	10.9
Stone Cutters' Association of North America, Journeymen	1,900	200	10.5
Metal Workers' International Association, Sheet	50,000	5,125	10.3
Asbestos Workers, International Assoc. of Heat & Frost Insulators &	10,000	1,003	10.0

Source: Laborer Organization in Canada, (Ottawa, 1957), p. 11; *Directory of National and International Unions in the United States, 1957*, Bulletin no. 1222, U. S. Department of Labor, (Washington, 1957), pp. 30-46.

TABLE 23
EARNINGS IN MANUFACTURING, 1939-1958—CANADA AND THE UNITED STATES

Year	AVERAGE HOURLY EARNINGS				AVERAGE WEEKLY EARNINGS			
	U. S. A.	Canada	Differential		U. S. A.	Canada	Differential	
	(Cents per hour)		Cents	Percent-age C/B	(Dollars per week)		Dollars	Percent-age G/F
	A	B	C	D	E	F	G	H
1939	64.6	42.2	22.4	53.1	23.86	20.14	3.72	18.5
1940	67.3	44.4	22.9	51.6	25.20	22.38	2.82	12.6
1941	77.0	48.9	28.1	57.5	29.58	24.94	4.64	18.6
1942	89.3	55.7	33.6	60.3	36.65	28.18	8.47	30.1
1943	98.8	60.6	38.2	63.0	43.14	30.82	12.32	40.0
1944	103.1	64.7	38.4	59.4	46.08	31.05	15.03	48.4
1945	98.5	66.4	32.1	48.3	44.39	30.74	13.65	44.4
1946	113.0	74.1	38.9	52.5	43.74	29.87	13.87	46.4
1947	125.8	85.1	40.7	47.8	49.97	34.13	15.84	46.4
1948	136.6	94.6	42.0	44.4	54.14	38.53	15.61	40.5
1949	139.2	98.4	40.8	41.5	54.92	41.71	13.21	31.7
1950	150.1	105.6	44.5	42.1	59.93	43.82	16.11	36.8
1951	161.5	122.2	39.3	32.2	64.71	48.82	15.89	32.5
1952	170.5	129.5	41.0	31.7	67.97	53.62	14.35	26.8
1953	178.0	135.9	42.1	31.0	71.69	56.09	15.60	27.8
1954	181.0	139.8	41.2	29.5	71.86	57.16	14.70	25.7
1955	191.0	144.8	46.2	31.9	76.52	59.25	17.27	29.1
1956	202.0	153.3	48.7	31.8	79.99	62.27	17.72	28.5
1957	209.0	160.5	48.5	30.2	82.39	64.64	17.75	27.5
1958 (June)	212.0	167.2	44.8	26.8	83.10	68.05	15.05	22.1

Source: Brecher and Reisman, *op. cit.*, p. 217; figures brought up to date.

INDEX

Abbott, D. C., 42 n.
Agriculture, Canadian: affected by U. S. policies, 81-87; wheat program, 73-75
Agriculture, U. S.: affects Canadian agriculture, 81-87; federal aid policy in, 69-70, 72, 73; surplus disposal program, 69, 70-71, 79-84
Aitken, Hugh G. J., 13 n.
Alberta: gas in, 27-32 *passim*; oil in, 22-27 *passim*
American Federation of Labor (AFL), 132, 133, 135, 147
American Federation of Labor-Congress of Industrial Organizations (AFL-CIO), 131, 132, 133, 134, 147
American Revolution, impact of, on Quebec, 91, 92
Anaconda Copper Company, 27
Arndt, H. W., 115 n.

Balance-of-payments, 106, 116
Bank of Canada, 58
Banking, 57-58
Barkway, Michael, 117 n.
Beveridge, Sir William, **59, 59 n.**
Bird, J., 36 n.
Blyth, C. D., 105 n.
Brecher, Irving, x n., 7 n., 8 n., **9 n.,** 11 n., 86 n., 102 n., 103 n., 104 n., 111 n., 113 n., 116 n., 119 n., 130 n., 136, 139 n., 140, 142, 153 n., 154 n., 156 n., 159 n., 160 n., 168 n., 171 n.
British Columbia; hydroelectric development in, 67; mentioned, 14, 24, 25, 95
British Commonwealth, vii, 147
British North American Act, viii, 127
Britnell, G. E., 69 n.

Canada, similarities and differences from U. S., vii-viii
Canadian and Catholic Confederation of Labour, 144

Canadian Congress of Labour (CCL), 131 n., 135
Canadian Copper Company, 16 ff.
Canadian development, U. S. need for, 44-45
Canadian Labour Congress (CLC), 131 ff.
Canadian Wheat Board, 74 ff.
Carty, E. B., 8, 8 n., 105 n.
Clark, Colin, 6, 6 n.
Cohen, J. L., 135
Congress of Industrial Organizations (CIO), 133, 135
Co-operative Commonwealth Federation (CCF), 135, 145
Crump, Norris, 131 n.

Davis, John, 26 n., 27 n.
Debt, national, 58-59
Depression of the 1930's, 52
Dexter, Grant, 32 n.
Diefenbaker, John G., 109 n., 123 n., 124 n.
Domestic output, industrial distribution of (table), 152
Drake well, 22
Drummond, W. M., 83 n., 167 n.

Earnings, manufacturing, of U. S. and Canada (table), 171
Easterbrook, W. T., 13 n.
Economy, development of: 4-6; post World War II, 37-48; future of, 64-66
Economy, influences on: 3-4, 6-9; American, ix, x, 9-13, 33-35, 39-50, 66-68 (*see also* Agriculture, Labor organizations, Industry, Investment); British and European 7, 8, 9, 37-38, 43
Economic policy, post World War II, 51-64